Small House

BIG DREAMS

An Urban Girl's Dream

LOMENKA BOURNE

ISBN 978-1-960546-98-2 (paperback)
ISBN 978-1-954345-35-5 (hardcover)
ISBN 978-1-960546-99-9 (digital)

Rushmore Press LLC
1 800 460 9188
www.rushmorepress.com

Printed in the United States of America

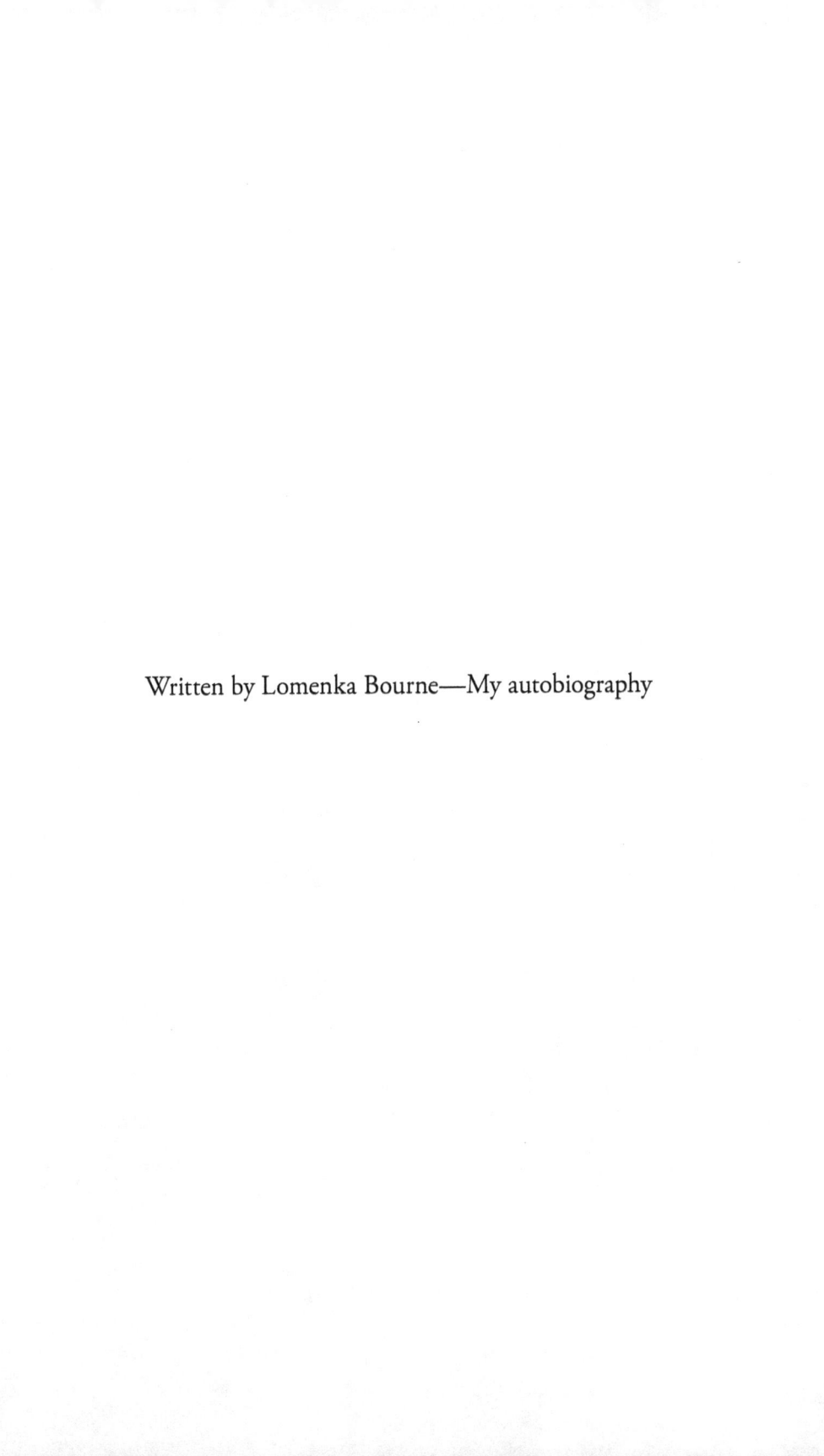

Written by Lomenka Bourne—My autobiography

The Opening...

"Facing ourselves is difficult but liberating. Half of the battle is denial. Once we find the courage to face the anchors which hold us back, we are well on our way into the self-discovery process. Likewise, we also need to find the strength to accept our wings and truly honor the potential they hold. An important touchstone in this process is connecting with, and revealing, our deepest hopes and dreams."—written by Hyde School Staff

This is a book about my life as a young African American woman. This book opens with a statement from a wonderful school called HYDE where it is said, "You are not responsible for the truth only seeking it."

"Taking builds confidence. Speak to the listening. Learn to take hold and learn to let go. Trust in the process."

I came to Hyde because of my teenage daughter. As a result of our Hyde education, I learned that I need to let go of my daughter's outcome, her future, and trying to determine her future. I have to ask myself the question, what risk do I take toward embracing my own unique potential? I need to let go of controlling the outcome because the harder I work, the luckier or blessed I get. My unique potential is a part of my spiritual power. My unique potential is not created; it is something that already exists in me.

This is my story about a child growing up in the streets of New York, Jamaica, Queens, an urban girl in an all-black family neighborhood with some poor white trash sprinkled around. As a child, I could not figure out where they came from and why they wanted to live with us. But I ignored them and treated them like everyone else did, as the White family that just happened to live in our neighborhood. I was cordial. I said hi and kept on moving.

Cultural Differences in the Late 1970s, early 1980s

One of the things that were very true about New York in those days was that everyone lived with their cultural group. We were true segregationists and we respected our places. We did not go around with hatred in our hearts for differences in culture—we celebrated Greek festivals, Italian festivals, Caribbean festivals, and Cuban and Puerto Rican festivals. Everyone came to the festivals. All were welcome and we partied like family, all races and all cultures. In New York, Jews and Blacks were kindred spirits and we related as if we were one. We felt each other's oppression and we joined together in the struggle to live with one another. We joined together as similar cultures in despair.

The contrast between the South and the East Coast was so different in the way the terms prejudice and racism were defined and the reactions to cultural differences. The South clearly hated black folks and had very little tolerance for other cultures as well. Segregation in the South was non-negotiable and it didn't matter whether there was a cultural event or not you stuck with your kind.

California in the early 1980s seemed to have a different flavor from the South; desegregation was a part of life. Neighborhoods were diverse. In California, segregation was around the color green, not culture. Don't think California was not prejudiced because it was. People masked their racist feelings by keeping up facades and pretenses. For example, every person at the bus stop speaks to all people with a kind word, a pleasant greeting, and sharing of social tidbits. The difference was if you asked them for a job or for business contacts or anything to do with housing or professional dealings, they would clam up. The proverbial "I'll be in touch" becomes part of the discussion and wait if you may but you may never hear a thing from them. Californians always seem to leave you thinking you have forged a friendship but it was only in the moment for the most part. It is their social hidden racism that is disconcerting, especially if you are not prepared for their subtle culture. New Yorkers, on the other hand, if you talk to them at a bus stop, they think you are crazy for the most part or you are setting them up for a con (some way to take them for their money). The cultural and social differences I have run into based on my travels are interesting and challenging based on the region of the United States you travel or live in.

FRIENDS & 1960 URBAN FAMILIES

We were all low-income families with small homes and most of us had two-parent households. Don't let that fool you. We all had things going on. One of my best friends had three parents: a stepmom, her biological mom, and her father. With all that family, she lived in her grandmother's house across the street. Her father, her stepmother, and two stepbrothers lived in the basement and her grandmother and her step-grandfather lived upstairs with her two adopted cousins.

Then there were my other best friends. They were sisters. They lived on my block. They lived with their biological mom, stepfather, and younger stepbrother and stepsister. Their biological dad lived about ten blocks away in somewhat of the same neighborhood. We called everything in our neighborhood. If we could walk to our friend's house or school without having to take a bus, then it was our neighborhood. Their father's mother and their grandmother lived next door to them. I considered it strange but then again, we all had crazy stuff going on.

My best buddy who happened to be a boy lived next door. He had the best household out of all my buddies. His biological mom and dad lived together in his mother's mom's house, his grandmother. He had a younger brother, Carl, who we would let play with us when we felt like it.

Then there was the family that moved from Harlem which we considered the ghetto, into the vacant house across the street. They had two boys and two girls. It looked like they had a mom and a dad but I can't remember their dad being around long. Their mom was a straight-up alcoholic and she gave them hell. My father was a drunk but I had never heard of or seen a mom as a drunk. Anyway, the two girls became my best friends. One of their brothers became the neighborhood thug. Their cousin who always seemed to visit was about ten years older than us and was a seasoned jailbird. That is what we used to call people who were in and out of jail in my day. He used to sit on the steps and tell us jail stories. He scared me to death. He would tell us about the gay life of pretty boys in jail and more. I knew I never wanted to be in jail. I decided from his stories that jail was not the place for me. The Harlem kids had another cousin who was mentally challenged. We called people like him retarded. Somehow, he liked me, not just as a friend. He really liked me. I was kind to him but I was really scared of him. He would follow me around the neighborhood in a stalking kind of weird way. He was creepy. It was creepy but the Harlem kids were my closest friends.

My mom's best friend lived a block away. I never understood their household. My mom's best friend lives with her husband and two daughters. She had some stepdaughters and a daughter from another relationship that did not live with them. Her husband was the first black entrepreneur I ever met. He owned a secondhand clothing and "what not" store. He collected stuff from everywhere and his store looked like that. His storefront was within walking distance, so it was in our neighborhood. Sometimes, my mom and I would go to his store and pretend we wanted to buy something. I would cringe every time my mom gestured to me and said, "Do you like this?" The store was so junky, I was always suspicious about where he got the store items from. My mom's friend's husband was mean. Whenever he came home which was all times of night and we were visiting, we quickly packed up our stuff and left.

You see, sometimes my mom and her friends would meet up to play cards until the late hours of the night. They would send us to bed while they played. My mom's best friend had two girls who were about one and two years younger than me. They had the biggest house in the neighborhood and sometimes, they would ask me to spend the night with them. I was happy since I didn't have a room of my own and they had their own rooms. I wanted to live like them. But I started to get scared of staying there. I would hear their dad yelling and screaming at their mom and watch him take a belt and whip her. While I hated my living situation, even as a child, I hated violence more. I wanted out of there. I tried to tell my mom but she would not listen. So, every time they asked me to stay I would make up an excuse and say no. Their family was weird. I remember a story about their brother dying in their backyard. A drunken man supposedly drove into their driveway where their brother was playing and rolled his car over him while he was riding his tricycle. That is the story we were told and if you ever saw the homes in my neighborhood with the long driveways leading to the backyards you would be a little suspicious too. They were just weird!

MY GRANDMOTHER

My Grandmother was the only grandmother I had and the backbone of my existence. She made my life doable. She was four feet eleven inches tall, a little tiny woman about ninety pounds with dark brown skin and long jet-black hair. She kept her hair in braids because she was so tender-headed. She hated to get it combed, so most times she wore silver-gray wigs. Her skin was smooth-like cotton. I can't remember seeing any wrinkles on her skin. She lived into her eighties. In her later years, she had diabetes and took insulin. But she loved to pick at her toenails, keeping them trim and clean but when you have diabetes, you have to be careful. She got an infection in one toe and it never healed. Gangrene set in and her foot and leg were amputated up to her knee. Before she could get used to the prostheses on one leg, the toes on the other leg began to show signs of open wounds that were not healing. Soon, her other leg had to be amputated up to the knee to stop the infection from traveling throughout her entire body. After the first amputation, my grandmother remained independent and learned how to walk using her prosthetics and began traveling again visiting my family and others by using public transportation. She called the city bus her private limousine which was usually very timely and got her where she needed to go. Not too much could hold my Grams down. She would get off the bus about seven blocks from our house because there was no real connecting service and she liked to walk; she would walk the seven blocks with her prosthetic leg. She was an amazing woman. She went back to school in her seventies to get her GED because she felt she finally had the time to get her high school diploma. They say I am a carbon copy of her and every time I hear those words, my chest sticks out and my eyes swell with such pride to even be considered close to someone who could follow in her footsteps.

She gave birth to five boys and adopted my aunt. She grew up in the South and eventually migrated to Brooklyn, New York. Her first husband died when she was pregnant with my father's youngest brother. She continued to raise her five boys. She brought her first home in Queens when my uncles were grown and had entered the armed services.

She wasn't going to have any of her boys hanging out on the street. They knew after high school the next step was the armed services. My grandmother was a pint-sized giant. She raised her boys to be men. She married a second time, a man I knew as Grandpa Charlie. He was the only grandpa I knew. My mom's dad died when she was a young girl and her mom died before him. As far as I can remember, Grandma never lived with Grandpa Charlie. He lived on one side of the town and she lived on another. We could walk to grandpa's house from where we lived but remember in Queens, New York. We walked everywhere as long as it never took us over an hour to get there. The buses ran everywhere but we could take shortcuts and beat the bus.

Anyway, Grandpa had a small house with a yard dog, but he had a lot of land around the house. He loved growing fruit and vegetables. I always loved picking grapes and figs from his yard. I would pick enough to take home but I would end up eating all of the figs while I went inside to sit and talk to grandpa. Grandpa was a quiet man. Whatever we asked him for, he gave us. He was easygoing and very mellow. Grandma would take the bus over to deliver meals to grandpa. When I went with her, she would stay and put his meals in the freezer and explain to him how to prepare them. She would check his refrigerator to see how well he was eating. She could tell how well he was eating by the meals that were left over from her last visit. She would begin to ask him questions about his day and how he was doing. He was so ornery with her and feisty. Sometimes, I would pretend I was doing something else and sneak and listen to them talk. My grandpa was so mild-mannered with us and so different from my grandmother, but their words never seemed to be spoken with anger. It was more like a language they had of their very own. When my grandmother would call us to leave for the day, my grandfather would say, "Why you gotta go? You know you can stay here with me," and my grandmother would say, "I got to get the kids home and get some sleep before work." My grandfather would call my grandmother by a pet name, and she would smile and keep moving out the door. Watching them sometimes made me sad, but I couldn't figure out why. I was just a kid and not in touch with my true feelings. I was so happy seeing them together, and I loved picking the fruit and playing in the backyard. My grandpa began to get very sick, and my grandmother checked on him more frequently until he passed away.

Grandma was a hard worker. She would clean houses in the early morning after she got off work from her night job. She owned her first house on Farmers Blvd and purchased a second home on 169th street. When grandpa died, she owned his house in Queens as well. She rented my grandpa's house out. The house she purchased on 169th street became my family's home and my dad's oldest brother's family's home. My grandmother said they were only supposed to live there for a short time until they each purchased their own home.

The house was a small two-family four-story home. One family section was about fifteen hundred square feet. It had one bath, kitchen, living room, two bedrooms plus a basement with two rooms, one of which was used as a bedroom. My uncle, his wife, and their two children lived in that family unit. The second family section was about one thousand square feet, a matchbox in size. It had one bath, living room, kitchen, one bedroom plus an attic with one room and that room served as a bedroom. This second family section is where my family lived my mother, my father, my two brothers, and me. My grandmother's house on Farmers Boulevard where I spent my summers was a one-family home with four floors and a large yard: formal dining room, living room, kitchen, television room, two bedrooms, plus an attic with two rooms that served as bedrooms. All of her family from the south moved into her house to jumpstart themselves on the East Coast. My grandmother took them all in, mostly her sister and brother's children. She took her sister in and her sister's daughter and her daughter and son. Then she took in her sister's sons of which there were about five. I don't know how many because I started to lose count. Her sister's sons were all alcoholics. They would drink until they fell out. My grandmother never said much about all of them taking over her house. It was like that was her mission in life to take care of her sister and her sister's children.

Sometimes, she would get a brother's child, but it was not often. My grandmother kept working and working. The summers at my grandmother's house were full of people. My father's youngest brother came to live with my grandmother; therefore, his three children were there every summer. I was there and my grandmother's sister's daughter and her two children were there as well. A few other cousins from my grandmother's brothers were there also. The house was full of people sleeping everywhere. My grandmother loved it. It was almost like the more, the better. We always seemed to have enough food and plenty of fun. I would go there instead of being sent to an away camp. My brothers never came with me because my parents sent them to overnight camp for most of the summer.

I loved my grandmother. I would wade through all those people to spend one-on-one time with her. When she came in from work early in the morning, I would wait for her to change her clothes and lie down. I would do a soft knock on her door and if she did not answer, I would go away. More times than not, she would answer almost anticipating my presence and say come in. I softly shimmied into her bed and lay beside her and asked her how her day was. She would tell me stories of the patients in the hospital that she had to take care of and she would talk about the white people's homes she cleaned. She would bring home clothes for us and all kinds of gifts from her maid jobs. Sometimes, she would stop at the Five and Ten store and buy all the girls dolls. I would ask her why she worked so hard and she would say, "Because I have to." Before I could ask another question, she was fast asleep. She would always tell us on her way to her room to wake her up by a certain time for work and you better believe I never forgot to watch the clock, but there were a lot of people watching the clock for grandma. I didn't quite understand the reasons why my grandmother worked so hard. I just knew it was the right thing to do and she was good at doing the right thing.

My grandmother and I were close. My other cousins were jealous of our relationship. My older cousin who I loved to hang out with who lived downstairs in our two-family home loved my grandmother and modeled her life after what my grandmother did for others. My cousin adopted everyone, and everyone was her cousin. When she married, she had one son born to her and four or five adopted children. Actually, I'm not sure how many adopted children, but she raised them all. Even with all my cousins' similarities to my grandmother, I was my grandmother's favorite. I bore her name and I displayed and exuded the essence of her. I was precocious, inquisitive, and driven even as a child, very much like my grandmother.

When the summers were over, my grandmother and I still talked almost every night. I would tell her of my parent's injustices and she would always make some sane excuse for their behavior that would make me feel less abused and picked on. Our relationship was so close that after my mother would whop me about something she thought I was doing, I would take the beating, and then I would come to my mother and ask her if I could call my grandmother to talk for a moment. My mother would say yes because my grandmother was like the mother my mother never knew because her mother died so young. Again, my grandmother would listen to me for minutes or hours whatever it took to make me feel better, and then say goodnight. Even though I told my Grams everything, I could not bring myself to tell of the sexual abuse I experienced from my brother. For some reason, I could not tell my grandmother about that. I think I thought it was my fault. I thought I was asking my brother to do those things to me because I was climbing into his bed. I could not bear the shame even with the woman I loved and adored the most in my life. I was too ashamed. How could I tell her that I was letting my brother do nasty things to me? She had taught me better than that. She was heavily into church and loved God and she raised me to love God too. How could I disappoint her and what excuse could I make to God? What made it worse was that there were times when my brother touched me it created weird, strange feelings inside of me that seemed like pleasure mixed with disgust and guilt. How could I explain this to my grandmother? I did not want her to call me a Jesuit child, a child of the devil. I did not want to lose our relationship. How could I tell her?

When the abuse escalated to my uncle who was living in my grandmother's house, he began telling us to sit on his lap while he gyrated and felt our breasts. The first time he did it to me and then his son began doing it to my cousins. I wasn't afraid to tell my grandmother because I saw that I was not the only one being abused and I couldn't stand for my only safe place to become unsafe. Somehow, I wasn't willing to continue to live a lie in my grandmother's house. It was my haven, my safe place, and I was not going to allow my uncle or his son to destroy it. I told my grandmother and she put a stop to it as best she could. They didn't touch me anymore but I think they continued, just that they wouldn't let my grandmother or I see it. So why couldn't I tell her about my brother? I tried, but the words would not come out. I was a nasty girl and I believed as a child my grandmother would not understand the truth because I didn't understand why I had mixed-up feelings. Something felt good and nasty. I was confused by my religious beliefs and my body's reaction. Instead, I asked her to ask my mother and father to move to a bigger house so that I could have my own room. I would still be scared but I thought maybe I could alleviate my fears by locking the demon out or keeping my light on all night, whatever, it didn't matter, but I would not sneak in my brother's bed anymore.

My grandmother began to talk to my mother about having my own room. My mom's solution was to make the living room my bedroom. The living room is the only community space in our little box house. Great! Now my dad and my brothers were mad at me because that was where the good television and stereo were. The living room was where we entertained our guests; my brothers couldn't bring them up to our room because it was my room too. My dad's cousins would visit him from time to time where they were going. Our kitchen could only hold three people at the table. My brothers and I would eat and then my mother and father would eat after we finished eating. After talking with my mom and hearing her response, my grandmother during one of our nightly phone discussions said, "Just come and spend the summers with me." I just cried. I knew we weren't going to move and I said okay.

My grandmother was my mom and my best friend. She would take time off during the summer to travel and I would travel with her. We would go South to North Carolina and to West Virginia. Sometimes, we would go by bus to Washington DC to see my grandmother's aunt's house. We were a traveling pair. Sometimes, we were joined by my grandmother's best friend who I called Auntie.

My Auntie was my grandmother's best friend. She was no kin to us, but my grandmother clearly loved her like a sister. My Auntie was so different from my grandmother. She was loud and a "gun-toting kill you" rather than "put up with your mess" kind of woman. She drove a Cadillac and the newest Cadillac every year for a while. She and my grandmother seemed to be around the same age. She was a black mulatto woman, red-skinned like an American Indian with long, wavy hair that she always wore in one or two braids, unlike my grandmother who wore wigs. When it was time to dress up and look presentable, my grandmother would put on a wig. She wasn't going to allow anyone to touch all that long-tangled hair. My Auntie on the other hand wore her hair out rarely but she loved to sport her long braids.

When we went to the South for summer vacation trips, my auntie drove my grandmother and me in the Cadillac. Once we hit the highway, she had a lead foot and she never drove less than eighty miles an hour, sometimes ninety. My grandmother sat up front, constantly saying to my Auntie to slow down but my Auntie would taunt my grandmother and me each time my grandmother asked her to slow down from speeding up. She knew how to shut my grandmother up and of course, I was clear that I was to be seen and not heard unless I was asked a question. I was scared especially when we hit the West Virginia Mountains, winding around that tall mountain. I remember the road winding and the altitude changing. My Auntie drove those mountains in that Cadillac like she drove the highway. I took my cue from my grandmother. If she stopped talking about her crazy driving, I figured she wasn't scared, so why should I be scared? We got there safe and sound and of course, my Auntie would turn to my grandmother and say, "You know I could drive this with my eyes closed." I didn't say anything to my auntie or my grandmother. I just thanked God that we were there and staying for a while before we had to drive on that winding mountain again.

My Auntie outlived my grandmother. She must have been about ninety when she died. I never got a chance to talk to her about her and my grandmother's relationship. I just know they loved each other and cherished one another in a very deep and profound way. When I visited my Auntie, she was not the same after my grandmother died.

MY FAMILY

And then there was me and my family. As I said earlier, I lived in a two-family house—two bedrooms, kitchen, living room, and one bathroom upstairs, and three bedrooms, kitchen, living room, and one bathroom downstairs. My uncle, his wife, and my two cousins lived downstairs. I lived upstairs with my mom, my dad, and my two brothers. My mom and dad had one bedroom and my brothers and I, the three of us shared one bedroom.

My family was no different from the rest of the neighborhood. We had our issues too. My father was known as the weekend drunk. My mother was thought of as a good woman who was raising her children while her husband was away in the armed services.

My mother was about five feet two inches tall, milk chocolate color, born from West Indian parents, Panamanian and Barbadian; she was the youngest of seven children all of whom were born in the West Indies. My mother was the only child born in Brooklyn, New York. My mother is and was beautiful. She had jet-long black hair as a child and was gorgeous as a teenager. My father's cousins and brothers always talked about my mother's beauty. My mother is in her late seventies and still holding her beauty today.

My mother's reputation was solid until my dad came out of the service and came home to live with us. Then things changed. My dad and my uncle (my dad's brother who lived downstairs) were treated with the utmost respect around the neighborhood. They knew everyone and everyone knew them. My mother's reputation took second to theirs.

My dad died in my first year of community college. My dad was super intelligent. He was a decorated secret service man. He graduated from high school at the age of sixteen and went into the service. He falsified his birth certificate to join there. My grandmother sanctioned it to keep him off the streets of Brooklyn. My dad grew up on the streets of Brooklyn. He worked his way up in the army and applied for duty in the secret service. He was given an intelligence position in the service and retired from the service with many medals of distinction. When he came home, he got a job in a large law firm in Manhattan. My dad was a man about five foot eight inches tall, had dark chocolate skin like my grandmother, was well built, and had interesting hair for such a dark-skinned man. His hair was wavy and somewhat straight without a perm. He had slanted black marble eyes that would get thinner and more slanted, almost oriental when he drank alcohol. He was a pretty man but not a womanizer. I would hear stories about my dad and his brothers and how my uncles were at parties with women, and they were all over the women but my dad was always somewhat of a loner. His way of partying wasn't with the women but with the bottle. I can't figure out whether that was because he was committed to his family or that was his nature. He met a woman in Germany before he married my mom and had a son, but once he married my mom, his childhood sweetheart, there were never any stories of other women in his life. Even after his death, the stories were about how women would go after him but how he wouldn't give them any energy but playfulness at the moment at the party. He always came home with my mom or to my mom. I guess as most girls do, I have spent my life looking for the image I have of my dad in a man, a male partner. I am sure he had weaknesses but to this day after his death, with elders left to tell the story, the story remains as told.

My dad went to work every day dressed in suits and polished shoes. He was the first businessman I ever knew in my life. He came home and read the newspaper, watched the news, and prepared his clothes for the next day's work. He would bring home exotic foods from Manhattan markets—eggplant, mussels, scallops, etc. My mother would prepare the foods just the way he liked them. Soon, he left his job in the city and got a job as a project developer, designing and assisting with the development of York College in Queens. My dad held it down during the week but when the weekends came, he was like a Jackal and Hyde. He had two different and very distinct personalities. He was hardworking during the week and drunk on the weekends. As he got older, he began to drink after work and on the weekends. In addition to drinking, he was always full of medication. He took so many pills; the dresser stand in his bedroom was filled with about fifty bottles of different medications. I still don't know why he needed so many drugs. I just know that every time he went to the naval hospital, or the military hospital, he came back with another set of medications. As I got older, I discovered that he was a diabetic and suffered from high blood pressure. The rest of the pills were never clearly known by anyone else but my father and his doctor. He would never let my mother go into the doctor's office with him. To this day, we assume he died of a heart attack. The doctor guessed that the shrapnel that was left from bullet fragments that were not removed from his body eventually tightened around his heart and killed him.

My brothers were older than me. My oldest brother was six years older than me, and my younger brother and I were eleven months apart. He is eleven months older than me. I also have a secret family brother. My dad's son was fathered in the service before he married my mom. My dad's son is German and about eight years older than me. My grandmother, my father's mother, snuck me a picture of him when I was about thirteen years old. My mom refused to talk about him. My dad would not talk about him either. My grandmother and I were also tight; we could talk about everything, but even she got a little silent when it came to my father's oldest son. About five years ago, in my forties, when I was home visiting my mom, a letter came in the mail addressed to mom from my stepbrother trying to locate his brothers and sister. It was weird. What were the odds that the letter would arrive during my visit to New York. After all, I had not been to New York for five years prior to that visit.

My Stepbrother's Letter

> *Dear Bernice Bourne,*
>
> *I am writing this letter for Tee Bo's. He is German and his English is not so that he could write this for himself. You probably already know about Tee Bo because he kept in contact with his Grandmother Lomenka Bourne for quite some time. As I am not sure as to what you know or do not know about Tee Bo's. I will try and tell you what I know. Tee Bo was born in Germany in 1946 and was conceived while T H was in the Army, stationed in Berchtesgaden Bavaria…*
>
> *When he learned of Thomas' our father's death and also learned about his three siblings, Tee Bo wrote back to me and said he would very much love to contact his siblings. This would mean very much to Tee Bo. He is an only child so has never had a father or brothers or sisters.*
>
> *Sincerely, Donald Dunn*
> *(Brother-in-Law of Tee Bo's)*

My mom was gracious enough to give me the letter and have me write to my brother. I say gracious because any discussion of my stepbrother was always silenced or ignored. I was so happy. As soon as I returned home, I pulled out my childhood photos, and there in the pile of pictures was my only picture of my stepbrother, Tee Bo's. He was about fifteen when he took the picture that my grandmother had given me so long ago. I longed to know him to find a person that was a part of me and a part of my father. Here out of nowhere is a letter from him where he was yearning for the same thing. I called him and wrote to him. It turns out he had made his first trip to the United States, California, fifteen miles away from my home at the same time I was in New York. I just missed him. But his daughter was here ten months later and I took my family, my husband, and my children to meet her. My niece spoke no English. Her boyfriend spoke English fluently and translated for us. I could not get over the strong family resemblance in the white complexion of the young lady who sat across from me, smiling and holding my hand. I wish it was my brother, who I had longed to meet all my life, but I was willing to settle for a part of him. We took plenty of pictures. It is hard for us to communicate in writing or to speak as he speaks little English, and I speak little German. I now understand why my father, of all languages, was fluent in German. More connections back to my childhood and my dad getting angry with us and speaking in German. Wow!

My brothers had no respect for my dad. You see my mom raised us. My dad did not come home to live with us until I was in my last years of middle school. By that time, my brothers were used to my mom and had very little respect for my dad. Don't get me wrong. They were afraid of my father. When he said move, we all moved quickly. We knew the deal. My father's voice and his hand did not play when it came to discipline.

My oldest brother couldn't wait to leave our home. He was dark chocolate, and by the end of high school, he grew to be about six feet tall. He had that Indian type of hair like my dad, jet black wavy and straight without a perm. The girls were in love with him. He was a track star. He ran and had medals for the one-hundred-yard dash, triple jump, and relay races. He won trophies in the nationals. He received a four-year college scholarship for track and field which my father encouraged him to pursue and take. He never finished college. This made my father furious. Instead, he married his high school sweetheart. My father hated but tolerated his wife. My brother had three children and became a New York Firefighter.

My youngest brother was more tolerant of my dad. He was good at the art of smoke screening. He would say the right things and be in the thick of trouble the entire time. He was afraid of my dad, but he learned the game and played it well. My younger brother was husky as a kid and very athletic. He was good at baseball, track and field, football, and swimming. He never stuck with any sport long enough to receive awards or a college scholarship.

When my younger brother entered high school, he lost all the extra weight. He was chocolate, about six feet two inches tall, and had the same hair as my father. The difference between my two brothers was my youngest brother was very charismatic no matter who he met. No matter their culture or their race, they all loved him. He was and still is a people person. The ladies loved his looks and personality. My oldest brother was just a pretty boy and he loved women. He was and probably still is a player. My youngest brother on the other hand never liked to abuse his relationships with women. He was with a lot of women but female exploitation and abuse were never his styles. My oldest brother to this day has ex-wife and new wife issues that are angled up in his exploitative treatment of women.

While women were not my youngest brother's issue, he was a rebel and always into something that bordered on some kind of trouble. When he graduated from high school, he wrecked my mom's first car. My brother went out joy riding while my mom and I were out. I think my father was home but drunk and passed out on the couch. It was funny because my mom and I came home and her car was parked on a different side of the street than where she left it. She began to question me and herself about where she originally parked the car before we left. As my mother approached the steps to our house, she started yelling about my father and his drunken behavior. She just knew my father went for a joy ride in her car under the influence. In a soft, faint voice, you could hear her under her breath talking about my father drinking and driving again. Everything was alright until she got closer and saw the physical damage to her car. My brother was slick enough to park on the other side of the street and hide the damage. When she noticed the damage, she went up the stairs hollering the entire time for my father and yelling at him. My father woke up in a daze asking her what happened. Soon, I could hear footsteps from my room coming down the attic steps. My brother's face was pale and for us dark-skinned folks, that is pretty hard to accomplish. He said, "Mom, dad didn't do it, I did." My mother couldn't believe it. You see, my brother didn't have a license and she didn't even know he knew how to drive. My brother was a true "undercover brother." That's not all. He would get in trouble in school and pay me not to tell. You see the teachers were tired of sending home notes with him and getting no response. So, his teachers sought me out as his sibling and the young innocent one to deliver the notes to my parents.

As he got older, before he graduated from high school, my brother started selling drugs in my parent's home. My brother and my cousin, the heroin addict/alcoholic, who lived downstairs, were my introduction to drugs. They would not let me take any hard drugs, plus I was a control freak—I needed to know what I was doing at all times. While I did not take drugs, I knew everything. I could recognize pills, weed, opium, and heroin. They would show me so that I knew the difference.

I remember hanging out across the street in the basement of my best friend's grandmother's house. She had three adopted cousins living with her grandmother. Once her dad and her stepmother moved out of the basement of her grandmother's house, her two adopted cousins moved into the basement. They got high and talked shit to each other. My friend and I were sometimes invited to join them because my brother didn't want me to talk about them doing drugs, smoking weed, and drinking beer and other alcohol. We just wanted to be in the know. They would never offer us any drugs, but they had some weed, some opium, and some angel dust. They had some reds and some other types of speed. Every once and a while, we would try some weed. I was afraid of hard drugs.

One time, we tried some weed laced with PCP–angel dust. The angel dust had me floating on air. I tried to walk to the corner store, which was three blocks away from the house, and I swear to this day, my feet never touched the ground.

My best friend, as we got older, started dipping and dabbing in hard drugs in high school. She used to invite me over to the drug table in the cafeteria to introduce me to the drug dealers and show me her stash. I was a control freak, and I wasn't interested in putting any drugs in my body that would make me lose control of my senses, but I loved being in the know. I hung out with all the hardcore people, but I was never a part of their shenanigans. They knew that about me, and we were still cool. My nerdy friends knew that about me, too, but they hung out with me because they wanted to be a part of some of it, but they did not want the stigma of being associated with hardcore street stuff.

After my father died, my brother got deeper into drug sales. He was arrested on a minor drug charge and they slapped his hand and let him go. Finally, his best friend moved out of state, and he moved with him. That was cool until he got arrested in the new state and instead of going to jail, he went into the service.

Through all of this, my youngest brother was still the best athlete I ever knew. He could outrun my oldest brother who had a track scholarship. He was great to watch on the basketball court. He would watch Dr. J and the other great NBA players and produce the moves on the street courts. My friends and I would hang around the basketball courts all the time to watch him and his friends play. Well, there was another reason. His friends were kind of cute and I was not going to pass up a chance to hang out with them. Even though my brother would not let any of his friends talk to me or me talk to them, I would manage to sneak in a "hey" every now and then. It was crazy because in the service, my brother became my dad. He went into the Marines and was a Drill Sergeant. He became a family man. He became a businessman and a weekend weed head. How ironic!

Then there was me. Up until age eight, I was small in stature, with long jet-black hair like my grandmother and my mom when she was a child. My mom kept her hair cut short when I was a child. I had eyes like my father. As a child, I looked like my father more than my mother. Around the age of nine, I began to pick up weight. During my pre-teens, I started losing weight because I would have to go with my brother to track practice and run around the track with the team. I hated it but it forced me to drop a few pounds. I picked up boobs early at the age of twelve and they grew bigger than some of my girlfriends. I had slimmed down a little, so I had a big butt, big thighs, a small waist, and big boobs. I don't need to say anything else. My saving grace was that I was a straight-up tomboy. I would sock a boy before I'd kiss him. Spin the bottle was very popular then and I worked on my reputation of becoming a good kisser. I was competitive that way besides not wanting to be labeled as the worst kisser on the block. I had to protect my reputation. A kiss was all the boys would get. My youngest brother taught me how to box. My father forced him to because I was getting beat up by the bullies when I was in middle school. After they kicked my butt, my youngest brother would go kick their butt and tell them he would be back for more if he heard of anybody messing with his sister. My youngest brother had a reputation in the neighborhood as a badass. Nobody, boy or girl, wanted to take him on. My father got wind of the fact that I was losing fights and made sure my brothers didn't let anyone pick on me. Then, he made them teach me how to fight. We had real boxing gloves and a punching bag. I got knocked out by my brothers a few times and I wasn't having that, so I learned how to fight. Once I knew I could kick ass, I became the tomboy bully. I started going into other people's neighborhoods where I didn't belong because even then, we had turf boundaries. My Harlem girlfriend neighbors and I weren't scared we were going to walk wherever we felt like. I had a mouth on me too. I learned how to curse from my brothers and his friends. My father when he got drunk would curse. Every other word he said was a curse word while I would get killed by my parents if they ever heard me curse. When I got outside with my friends, the bad ones, that is, I would let go of my conservative, good-girl language and get into my street side. Everyone who knew me understood it was not a good idea to get me mad. I would make you feel like you were the last piece of scum on earth when I got finished cursing you out. I like my younger brother, Jackal and Hyde. I had two faces, the quite innocent shy girl my parents spoke so highly of and the street hood tomboy who took no mess and gave out a lot of her own. Depending on the friends I was hanging out with, I would display either side of my dual personality.

I was the apple of my father's eye. I was my mother's worst nightmare because she only wanted two children. I was an unwelcome surprise that she tried all kinds of home remedies according to my aunt, her sister, to get rid of.

My mother got used to me and began to treat me like a doll. I wore the best clothes and for a ghetto child, had about fifty pairs of shoes, but like it or not, I was a tomboy and a church girl. I could climb the trees, jump the fences, and get in your face with the best of them. I was a shit talker but funny, shy, and all business. To the world, I was a tomboy with a body to die for. I had long black hair straightened with a hot comb. It was down past my shoulder blades. My body was developing at the age of nine and I was fully developed by the time I was twelve. To my brothers, I was known as the banker. When no one else had money, I did. I started out lying and cheating to get money. But I still remember, at about nine years old, stealing my uncle's electric and gas money to pay his bills and taking it upstairs to my room, and placing it in my bank for saving. I will never forget my uncle's expression when he found out it was me who stole the money. I was his favorite niece and I saw the disappointment in his eyes. He said he would give me whatever I wanted but never, ever steal. That wasn't enough. I got the worst butt whip and punishment. But the biggest and worst thing was that my whole extended family knew I was stealing. Whenever we would go to our family gatherings, which we did every holiday, I was the talk of the group. I got the crazy eye from everyone. I was so embarrassed. I was cured for life.

CHILD ABUSE/BEING MOLESTED

I started growing breasts early. I think I was about nine when my breasts started coming. I had a horrible skin disease, eczema, and on top of my skin problem, I was developing as a woman. I was scared and I grew shyer and more introverted. My oldest brother was about fifteen and starting to date girls. He and his friends spent time on the stoop talking about girls all the time. I could hear their conversations.

I was always a scared child too. My brothers would want to turn out the lights all the time to watch scary movies. Then they would pretend they were going to the bathroom and sneak up the attic stairs and scare the hell out of me. I couldn't sleep at night. Even though my brothers were in the same room as me, I was still scared. I would sneak into my oldest brother's bed and take shelter in both of us being together if something came up the stairs to get us. My brother instead of kicking me out of the bed would begin to feel my body and touch me in places that were not appropriate. He would tell me shhh! Don't tell anyone. Soon it became a routine for him. He would experiment on me and then try it on his girlfriends. I did not mind because he kept the boogeyman away. While there was no penetration, I felt nasty. I knew it was wrong. I was only nine years old. When I would try to get in bed with my mom, she would send me back to my bed. I was scared! My brother would hear me coming up the stairs and call me to his bed. As I grew older, I realized that I could not do this. So, I began writing letters to my mom and sneaking them on her dresser for her to find and read. The more I would write to her, she would act as if I never said anything. We never discussed the letters. I became more and more blatant. I began putting them in her room during the day for her to read but still, she ignored them.

The letters would read...

Dear Mom,

I'm afraid at night and I went to sleep with you but when you turn me away. I go to my oldest brother's bed and he touches me in places that are not good... I want you to tell him to stop ... I want my own room. I'm afraid of the dark...

I wrote and read this letter to my mother as a 40-plus-year-old adult...

Dear Mom,

I always wondered why I spent so much time hating you. I loved my dad. He was my hero. I never knew if you loved me, but I always knew you loved my oldest brother. Your love for him showed without hugs, kisses, or "I love yous." I wonder if you sacrificed me to protect your relationship with him. I used to be angry with you. My father wanted you to move our family to a bigger house so that we could have more room as a family. My father sobbed when he talked about your unwillingness to move. I was a young child watching a grown man cry. He had his G.I. bill and he wanted more than our tiny house for his family. He cried to me. He told me how you spent the money he would send you not just taking care of us but on your brothers and sisters. Why mom? They were older than you and they could take care of themselves. Why did you do that? Was it because they raised you after your parents died? Did you feel obligated to repay them? What was going on? Why couldn't you talk to Dad about it?

My father said it was because you did not want to clean a big house and that you did not want the burden of a big house once everyone was grown. How selfish you *were. It wasn't just that Dad said this. I remember asking you to move to a bigger house. I remember convincing grandma to ask you to move to a bigger house. I remember grandma telling me that the house we were in was meant to be a starter home for Dad and his brother. Grandma purchased the house but she never intended for Dad and you to stay there after my younger brother was born. Dad didn't either but you changed the plan. You were a very selfish woman.*

The only people you cared about then were my oldest brother and your siblings. Your siblings were your first love and your firstborn was your second love. When my younger brother was born, you were angry, but you accepted the pregnancy and the birth of your second son. When you were pregnant with me, you tried several times to abort me. Your sister, my Aunt, made it clear to me that I was not the chosen child. It's okay because God had a bigger plan as has been revealed to you in your old age. It is ironic that I am your best child, your protector, your financial provider when needed, and your support system through hard times.

Mom, I am not done yet. I still need to understand you more. I want to know how you could choose your family over Dad. I want to know how you could choose my oldest brother over me.

I spent my young teenage years through college and until I had my family hating you. Because of the things my dad and grandmother shared with me about your choice not to move. You see, I could not conceive of a woman who would leave her two sons and her daughter in the same bedroom and think that it was the right thing to do, especially when there was a choice that could have been made to change the situation.

Secondly, I could not understand why you choose to ignore my letters concerning the incest that was occurring in your house with your children. The part of the letter you chose to respond to was about finding another place for me to sleep. You suggested that I move into the living room where I would have no privacy. It had no door. My brothers and my father were angry about the choice you had given me. They were not angry at you but at me for taking away the <u>only</u> community/social living space in the house, that was an unacceptable choice for me to make! How could I choose the living room space given their anger and the fact that there would be no privacy? Even my father said no. You set the situation up to fail. All the time rejecting my father's repeated attempts to buy a bigger house.

I didn't tell Dad about the sexual abuse. He just quit the service and came home to live with us. I did not want him to leave me again. I knew he would kill my brother if he knew what he had done to me. You didn't tell Dad either because you wanted to stay where you were and you did not want to give him an excuse to buy another house. You pretended to be passive and subservient, but you were controlling and manipulating the show at any and all costs.

You sacrificed me to hold on to your selfish desires. I hated you and when dad died, I waited long enough to get accepted into a four-year college to move away from your selfish, controlling, passive ways.

As for my oldest brother, there is a God. He became the same selfish controlling person you were. He is your son. He began to use his ways against you. He accepted your love and your gifts, but after he controlled your giving and he got what he needed, he left you; he verbally abused you, left you in financial ruin, cursed you, and vowed never to speak to you in his lifetime. What poetic justice. I feel vindicated in a sad, sadistic way.

God is a just God.

Somewhere, the tables turned, and I began to forgive you. Perhaps, it's my acceptance of God in my life, or perhaps it's my ability to forgive myself for the things outside of my control. I don't know. I just know I forgive you and I love you.

Mom, today when I look at my divorce, I realize I was you. I was the passive subservient manipulative wife. I was controlling the show from behind the scenes. I thought I was different because I didn't sacrifice my children but I did sacrifice them and my adopted children by giving them only what I thought was enough to keep them happy and keep their dad in my life. They loved me and I loved them for the sake of family. God blessed me to learn to love each of them from my heart, not just to keep my family together. Now I am looking back on two stepchildren I raised whom I barely talk to and for the first time, I understand that I am a reflection of you. How sad, how very, very sad. I still have work to do.

Me, Your Only Daughter

My father finally came home to live with us, and my brother stopped using me as a guinea pig for what he was going to try on his girlfriends. I was afraid to tell my father. I knew he would kill my brother. My youngest brother and I fought all the time. So, talking to him was like talking to my worst enemy.

I began to question my dad about moving. He would cry out of nowhere sometimes and say things in his most alcoholic moment that made me understand things about my mother that were not good. I was a very intelligent child, precocious, and my dad was sharing things with me that were for adult conversations but I was my dad's best friend in our home. I knew things about my mom that devastated me. I knew why she refused to move to a bigger house and get me out of my brother's bed. I begin to hate my mom. She was selfish. She was going to take care of her biological family before she would take care of and honor me and my dad. I began to hate her and her brothers and sisters. I kept asking my dad at different times the same questions and I would ask the questions in different ways until the same answer would arise from his lips. He would say, "I sent plenty of money home from the service to your mom to make a better life for my family and she gave it to her family. I want you to have your own room. I want us in a larger home but your mom..." I was a child who understood more than I was ready to deal with. I could not hurt my dad by telling him what my brother had done to me. I did not want him to kill my brother, hurt my mother, and leave me again. I suppressed the pain and so did my dad. You see, for the first time in my life, I understood one of the reasons why my dad drank so much.

MY DETERMINATION
TO SUCCESS

Despite all of this, I grew more determined to be successful. I knew that I was going to have a family and I was not going to become my mom. Then came high school. It was 1970, the beginning of integration in New York schools. Rioting, name-calling, "Nigger," and traveling miles and miles to high school became a part of my life. Woo, those were deep, crazy times. I was thirteen years old, somewhat excited about going to high school, and a little scared because while I could talk a good game about being a teenager, I did not know what to expect from the big kids.

You see, in Junior High school, IS72 was not a piece of cake. I had to fight my way through bullies. My father had to come to school for me because I was showing off in class and believe me, that was not a pretty sight. My dad didn't play when it came to education. He had just come home on leave and the teacher was calling him to come to school for my out-of-control behavior. The teacher said, "I was climbing on the window like a monkey." In truth, there were no window poles in the classroom to open up the window so I, with my tomboyish self, decided to climb up on the window ledge to get a grip on the window to open it. The only problem was the teacher had no control over the classroom and I was adding to the problem by helping my fellow classmates out, by getting some fresh air into the room. It was my first and last detention slip. My father went off in front of the class and embraced me. He let the teacher and my classmates know who was in charge. After that night's whooping and the fact that the embarrassment of my father's visit did not look so good, the next day at school, the kids teased me and I was through with showing out. Besides, I had already felt left out because my best friend and I had been in the same classes in elementary since we were in kindergarten. When we went to middle school, my best friend was put in a smarter class than me and that made me feel stupid and out of place. We were separated into two classes. The class I was in seemed to be full of hardheads and bullies. I hated it. I had to learn to get mine and ignore them but act like I was a part of them to keep them off me. I fought the bullies to establish my place but I hated every minute of it. I used to walk to and from school. Almost every day, there was a fight on the street corners on the way home from school. My brothers had a reputation in the neighborhood for being some kick-ass fighters and I lived in their reputation. If I didn't win the fight, my brothers were sure to come and retaliate and make sure the neighborhood understood that you don't mess with our family. Soon, the fights stopped. The bullies began to pick on the easier targets and left me alone.

While I did not get in trouble in school anymore, my new friends in the neighborhood from Harlem were cool. They did not start anything but they knew how to finish something. I was a hardcore tomboy and I walked the streets like I could do anything a boy could do, including whip ass. After getting beat a few times, my brothers taught me how to fight and I was prepared for whatever. We were territorial back then. Our neighborhoods were based on how far we could walk without getting on the bus and they were set by school boundaries. In middle school, our boundaries were the distance between the two middle schools in our neighborhood (IS72 and IS8). The schools were about twenty city blocks apart. A city block is about a school track around. We would break school boundaries by walking to the other school just to see what was up and meet some new friends. We knew the deal and as soon as we got close to the school, we met up with some girls hanging out on the stoop and the looks started. If you didn't get what's up, you got a stare-down. Soon after the stare-down came the confrontation. We were down for whatever. I was Ms. Mouth. I could talk about all kinds of mess. Again, I was not out to start anything but if you went there, I was going there with you mouth and all. I would purposely walk with my hair braided into one long braid and with Barbie pins to pull it up so nobody could get a real grip on my hair if we started fighting. Sometimes, we wouldn't finish it then but we would come back on another day to let them know we were not scared and we were going to walk wherever we wanted and whenever we felt like it. Those times, we would have our Vaseline ready. You couldn't get a grip if you were slippery. It gave the greasy fighter the edge.

Walking the neighborhoods, cooking, packing our lunch, and heading for Jones Beach, playing skully in the streets, jumping double Dutch, playing stickball, practicing the latest dances, singing the latest R&B hits, and corn rolling hair was how we spent our spring breaks and our summers up until sophomore year in high school. Then things changed. Boyfriends, my commute so far to high school and summer jobs changed my ability to hang out with my friends the same way. I started working when I was fourteen. I worked at a church bible school and with summer camps as a junior camp counselor. I had to work because I loved money. In the winter, I used to sell my father's complimentary New York Knick tickets from his job. My dad never went to the games, but he would have at least six-floor level complimentary ticket seats that he would get from his job. He never went to the games and I would hustle my father for the tickets before my brothers got wind of them. One of my best friends was a boy, "my buddy" in the neighborhood. He and I were a team, the neighborhood hustlers, and entrepreneurs. My mother brought me a potholder maker craft kit. I would make potholders and crochet skull caps. My grandmother taught me how to crochet, and we would have my dad's Knick tickets. We sold the Knick tickets for half of their face value. After we built a regular clientele, I taught my buddy how to make potholders so that we could increase the number of potholders we had for sale. We had regular customers. Now that I think about my buddy, he and I were pretty close. We broke the gender lines. We were all about the money.

My mom and dad were pretty popular in the neighborhood. Their church friends and their neighborhood friends were our customers. My buddy and I would ring their doorbells on a regular basis to sell tickets, potholders, crochet skull caps, and scarves. My buddy was my backup, my protector, and the person who helped me get my nerve up to ring the bell. We agreed on a fair cut of our sales monies. When business was slow in the winter, we would shovel our neighbors' yards, only the ones without kids for money. The neighbors with kids would always want to use us as an example to make their kids get up and shovel the snow. We pissed off a lot of our friends because their parents would make us the good guys and them the lazy no-good kids. Needless to say, we stayed away from our friends' homes.

We were true entrepreneurs before we knew what the word meant. I was known as a banker for a reason. I would save for my school clothes and of course my shoes for each school year. I was a shoe fanatic. My mom always worked at a department store where they sold children's and young adults' clothes. She would get an employee discount on our clothes, so my brothers and I would be set for school with new clothes every year. She would start shopping at the end and the beginning of every season. At the end of the season, she would catch the sales. She would shop at the beginning of the season to catch the newest arrivals. It was really cool. That wasn't enough for me. I needed more; I always had a fetish for kit leather shoes. There was a designer store in Manhattan called the "Glove Shop." The Glove Shop had the baddest—leather flats in all kinds of designs. The toes of the shoes were cut in geographic shapes, some tied on the side, some had an elastic slip-on, and some had stylish buttons, but they were all in leather, different colors, and expensive fifty dollars a pair. They were pretty expensive but I was determined to have more than one pair for the school year. That store was my store. My mom took me shopping there once when I was about twelve years old. My mom believed in us wearing expensive shoes that would protect our feet. Even though we had two pairs of shoes when we were younger, they were the best shoes her money could buy. As I got older, I wanted the more stylish best shoes so I started to venture out beyond Queens to find them. I would take buses and the train to shoe stores that had unique styles of leather shoes. I would see people with shoes that I liked and ask them where they got them from. I would write down the address or the approximate location and ask my uncle who lived downstairs how to get there. My uncle worked as a train conductor on the New York City trains. He knew how to get everywhere. He was a walking transit map. He would tell me how to get where I wanted to go and I was off on my way. I didn't need anyone to come with me because I didn't want anyone to steal my style. We didn't have cell phones then, so if I got lost and I did, I was just lost. Getting lost was rare because my uncle had the train system down. I was only lost when the trains were so crowded that I could not see my stop and I missed it and had to jump off and catch the next train back. Sometimes, I was in some awful spots, especially when I was in the Bowery then the homeless pit of Manhattan. The subways there and in the South Bronx were the worst. Just like a New Yorker, I was cool, hardcore in the face, and non-interested in the things going on around me. I didn't speak to anyone and I looked like I dared anyone to speak to me. My grandmother had told me about the street hustlers. I watched people get hustled. I overheard my uncles talking about how they had been hustled and they were pretty street smart. You see, my mom and her brothers grew up in Brooklyn, Bedford Stuyvesant, in the hard-core area of Brooklyn. If they could get hustled, I knew that I could too. I loved shoes so much that I was willing to save my money to buy them and travel all over New York to find them. I still have a passion for shoes. It is a little tempered. I don't have one hundred pairs of shoes but I still cannot resist a jazzy pair of shoes.

Boys, boys, and more boys started entering my atmosphere. I was a tomboy. I was known as a tomboy. It was hard to shake that image. I had bad skin rashes. I didn't know what to do with boys who liked me except to smile and look. I was not a good girlfriend. I would beat them up if they said something off the wall to me. I lost a boyfriend to my best friend because I was just mean. I would kiss him and fight him. Crazy stuff! When I found out my Harlem neighborhood friend was his new girlfriend, I was hurt. I screamed at her and him and then decided that he wasn't worth it. Somehow, I realized that I didn't like him that much and they looked better together than he and I did. It was strange, but after a little bit of time, my girlfriend and I became friends again. I think it was because he became annoying to her and we both saw him for what he was which was not very much. I learned a valuable lesson. I think in my head even as a young girl I knew that I never wanted to fight or argue with a woman over a man. I got that if he could do that to me, what makes me want him in my life anyway? Especially because after my ex-boyfriend broke up with my girlfriend, he tried to talk to me again. I almost fell for it but even at fourteen, I knew to beware. I was suspected of that kind of behavior. It seemed too easy, plus I asked my younger brother's advice (when we weren't fighting, he was actually pretty cool). He said, "Let him go. He's not worth it. He is just trying to teach you a lesson or rebounding, saving face." My brothers taught me a lot about men either by watching them dog out women or asking my younger brother questions and sometimes just ear hustling, listening to my brother's friends talk about girls as they sat on the steps while I was braiding their hair.

BEING A TEENAGER CHANGING, MATURING, GROWING UP

Something happened and I started becoming very self-conscious of my body and my skin. I guess my hormones were raging. I started eating more and more and I got heavier and heavier. Boys were still interested but I became overwhelmingly shy. I did not like the street corner human whistling and the cat calls. I didn't have the tomboy image anymore. I wanted what the other girls had, boyfriends. I became afraid of boys outside of my childhood buddy that I grew up with and my brothers. I begin to see boys less as hang-out buddies and more as wanting to be a couple, in a relationship. You know the boyfriend/girlfriend thing. The more I worried about it, the more my skin allergies flared up and the heavier I got. My skin allergies were best in the winter when no one could see that they were clearing up. As soon as the seasons changed from winter to spring, spring to summer, and summer to fall, I got my Junior High School nickname "Itchy Ball." With the sun and my skin rashes, my body was darker in the summer than my already milk-chocolate skin. Behind my knees was dark, my skin was black in the crease of my arms, behind my neck was black, and yes, my face was the prime target for bumps and a scaly peeling rash. The hotter and more humid it got, the worse my skin allergies were. And with all that going on, I had the nerve to want a boyfriend and to be entering high school. I was messed up. My brother's friends were still my buddies and my childhood boy buddy/business partner hung in there with me no matter what I looked like on the outside. He was so cool. I just knew I was going to marry him. We hung tough together. High school kind of changed our mix and as we got older, we grew apart. He ended up committing suicide. He blew his brains out with his own gun.

Integration happened and my buddy's parents decided they weren't going to send him fifty miles away to high school in an all-white area. Busing was out for him. However, my parents thought it was alright for me. My dad even in his most drunken state, would wake us up for all and any black history television programs to make sure we understood our ancestry and our black history. He wanted me, not my brothers, to have the best education possible and he knew it was available in the white schools, in the white neighborhoods. My brothers were athletes. My oldest brother already had a full-track scholarship before the integration of New York schools from our neighborhood high school and my younger brother was equally as athletic. My younger brother was a budding basketball and track star. Because of my oldest brother's athletic performance, his coach made arrangements for my youngest brother to attend the same high school. So, my youngest brother managed to escape "busing." Not me, I was the "sacrificial lamb."

RACISM SCHOOL DESEGREGATION IN NEW YORK

The civil war began in 1861 and ended in 1865. Brown vs. the Board of Education was in 1954. In 1957, Little Rock 9 went to central high school in Little Rock Arkansas. Why was New York so far behind the times?

School Desegregation and Prejudice in the United States

By
Mary Ellen Leahy

"Also, in 1969, Alexander v Holmes (Mississippi) Board of Education ordered school systems to integrate no later than February 1970. Eventually, this deadline was extended for years. In that same year, the Court, in Carter v. West Feliciana Parish School Board, scolded the school board for delaying student desegregation.

"In 1970, the Supreme Court decided Swann v. Charlotte-Mecklenburg (Virginia) Board of Education. This was the first decision made by the Supreme Court during the Nixon administration with the two new Chief Justices who were Nixon appointees. In this first decision, written by Chief Justice Warren E. Burger, one of President Nixon's nominees, the court found Charlotte-Mecklenburg out of compliance with Green. The Court adopted the Finger Plan, a plan proposed by Dr. John Finger, an expert witness in the case selected by the Court. The Finger Plan was to result in schools throughout the

system ranging, ideally, between nine- and thirty-eight percent black enrollment. These percentages were not absolute but a goal. It involved busing an additional thirteen thousand students and buying over one hundred new school buses. Start-up costs to implement this plan were over one million dollars, with annual operating expenses of over one-half of a million dollars. Swann v. Charlotte-Mecklenburg laid the framework for all future court decisions involving busing. It also implemented the Green decision. Basically, it said that if a school district is found to be in constitutional violation, an appropriate remedy must be implemented. In 1974, the Swann case was closed, leaving the constitutional operation of the schools to the Board of Education"

It is the 1970s in New York. The civil rights movement is alive and strong. Segregation of schools was abolished.

"In 1970, Senator John Stennis of Mississippi and other Southern Senators proposed that new federal desegregation guidelines be enforced uniformly across the country. The Stennis amendment was adopted by the Senate. During the 1960s, urban schools in the north and the south were untouched by the courts. The Courts had been concentrating on the rural South. The 1960s had seen great migration of rural Southern blacks to Northern cities. In the early 1960s, three-fourths of all blacks in the United States lived in urban areas. The north had its own way of distancing blacks, ghettos. In the South, there was de jure segregation of schools, which is segregation of schools required by law. In the North, there was de facto segregation of schools, which is segregation of schools due to residential segregation."

New York's answer to desegregation and integration was "busing." I was in the heart of it. I went to the only new Middle School built in Jamaica, Queens in 1967 which was a beginning attempt to look at blacks and whites possibly attending the same schools by creating new facilities.

Then there was the remapping of school districts in an attempt to take children from New York black segregated neighborhoods and place them in white-segregated neighborhoods. Growing up, and still somewhat true today, people in New York borough by borough live in neighborhoods according to their culture. Even blacks were defined by their culture. Haitians lived in Haitian communities, West Indians lived in West Indian communities, and people of direct African descent lived according to their region and stayed in separate communities based on their culture. This extended to everyone including whites; Italians lived in Italian neighborhoods. When it came to Hispanics in New York, there were only two kinds: Puerto Ricans and Cubans and because of the language barrier, we weren't sure how they handled their cultural differences but we could only guess. You see, we lived with both cultural tolerance and discrimination.

Busing to me was about blatantly taking blacks out of their inferior education neighborhoods and placing them in all-white areas where their schools never experienced a black student or a black teacher. This was more than a thirteen-year-old from Jamaica, Queens was ready to handle. I was going through hormone changes, physical changes, seasonal skin rashes, and an identity crisis; am I a tomboy or a girl? I was messed up and totally unprepared for a bunch of red-neck white people who didn't want change. They did not want niggers living next door and certainly did not want them going to school with their children.

The first day of school... I worked hard that summer. I have on my new shoes and my best clothes. After all, I was going to see boys, new boys that did not know me. I did not know them too. Time for a new beginning and the possibility of a boyfriend of course. My friends and I met at the corner and walked to one of the identified bus stops. Yes, we had to take the yellow bus to school. When we arrived, there were about six buses waiting patiently for us to load up. We were like cattle being herded and corralled for a new destination. Well about thirty-five minutes later, we arrived. The school was large, and the neighborhood was quiet and still except for the campus. We had a welcome of people parked across the street with shotgun shouting all kinds of things. It was hard to hear everything over the armed police standing in the street between the park across the street where all of the angry white folks were camped and the school building. The police were armed with shotguns and tear gas. Rows and rows of police and white people loaded up in a one- or two-mile radius park. You could hear a pin drop on my bus. We had never seen anything like it. We were scared and confused. I remember just wanting to go home but I did not know how to get there because this was my and everyone's first trip to this foreign place. We couldn't walk to the bus stop and go home. Hell, we didn't know if we were still in Queens. It was like someone had kidnapped us and left us stranded with people standing around waiting to kill us. In order to call home, we had to first get into the school building. How were we going to do that when the police were busy holding off the angry white folks and it didn't look like it was going to stop anytime soon? So, we sat, and finally, the police were able to gain control over the crowd. But instead of entering the school, we were sent home only to return the next day with a promise of guaranteed order. Our parents were products of the civil rights movement. They watched the student riots for equal rights on college campuses and they were firm believers in Martin Luther King and John F. Kennedy. There was never any discussion about our not going back the next day. Our parents were up earlier than we were to make sure we were at and on the bus on time. I remember my father saying, "These white folks are not going to keep us out of nothing anymore. You go there and walk with your head held high. The police are there." He said, "Those white folks are mad but they aren't crazy enough to take on the police." My dad was right. This time, we got on the bus and we were rowdy for the first part of the ride but as the bus grew closer to the school, there was airy silence. After we got off the freeway, we took the first turn and the second turn and finally the last turn... We saw the park and then the school.

The park had fewer people and this time, there were no guns. They traded their guns for picket signs. Somehow, they adopted a peaceful protest mode which was less scary but still unsettling. This time, the police were not lining the street but patrolling the area on foot and on horses. Guns were not drawn on either side. We were escorted off the bus by teachers, administrators, and police officers. As we walked toward the massive school building that we had only seen from the outside, a new fear began to set in. We had not met the students or any of the teachers and had not received a tour of the school. We walked into a high ceiling old cathedral-style building. The school was old but well-kept. The outside was brick and mortar. The inside was cold and you could hear echoes in the hallways. Welcome to high school.

After a week or two of police escorts, the white folks grew tired of their protest and each day, there were fewer and fewer people in the park. The students were less hostile than their parents. They kept their distance but were very curious and so were we. When we ate in the cafeteria, we had our section and they had theirs. As time went on, we became more of a melting pot inside, student to student. The teachers and the neighborhood parents shared the same view of what they thought we were. Believe me, we weren't held in high regard. My friends did not help. They were complete idiots at times. They were disrespectful, rude, and unruly. To my surprise, there were drugs all around the campus and we weren't the ones bringing them to the campus. Once things settled down and the police left the campus, a student culture began to evolve. For the most part, the black kids were treated inferior by the teachers, counselors, and administrators. When it came to the students, everyone began to find their own niche. New York culture began to take hold. Drugees with drugees, science club with science club, socialites with socialites, and jocks with jocks... Soon, just like water when you keep adding it to a container and stop, it will find a balance and level off; the students did the same. The color of our skin was still an unspoken issue but in the confines of the school, we were all just different, but people. This was not true for the teachers and the guidance counselors.

My father was determined for me to go to college which meant that I was not on a general education track but on a college-bound academic track. He made a one-and-only visit to the school on a forty-five-minute public transportation bus ride to ensure that everyone from the principal of the school to the guidance counselors understood his academic goals and intentions for me. They followed his orders and placed me in Algebra, Geometry, Pre-Calculus, Biology, and General Physics and of course, three years of foreign language classes. I was the only black person in most of the above classes in my sophomore, junior, and senior years. I struggled and my father struggled with me. He would help me type my reports, review my math assignments with me, and help quiz me for my exams. Even with all his support, I struggled. I couldn't join student study groups because the yellow buses stopped running after 4:00 PM and during the winter months, it would get dark around 5:00 PM. A young black girl could not be caught on a street corner in a lily-white neighborhood after dark. Besides, when the yellow bus took us home, it took about thirty to thirty-five minutes depending on traffic. If I took public transportation during rush hour, it may take forty-five minutes, but during non-peak hours, it could take me over an hour and a half to get home. Needless to say, staying after school for tutoring or to meet with a teacher that was not racist and wanted to help was almost impossible. Early morning, after school, and weekends were out of the question because of the tension in the surrounding neighborhood and the blatant racism. So, I struggled but I refused to quit. Sometimes, I would get "Fs" and I would have to repeat the class because I just couldn't get it. But I would hear my father say, "You deserve the same education as those white folks. Don't let them rob you of your education." I kept on pushing right through the humiliation, the silent snickers by the white boys who had no problem understanding the materials, and the laughs and cocky smiles of the teachers who kept saying I didn't belong there, but I knew my father would have their jobs if they messed with me. I kept on pushing because I was going to prove those white folks wrong. I knew if my father was as smart as he was and I was a part of him, I could do it. Besides, I hated guns and white folks angered me by thinking they were better than me because of the color of my skin or lack of color in their skin. I hated racism and I hated white folks. I was so determined to show them, to prove to them that a black girl from Jamaica, Queens could make it despite their efforts to keep her down. I still remember meeting with my guidance counselor in High School, my junior year, and her telling me not to even bother applying for four-year colleges because I would not be accepted. She told me to go to a junior college. She said I did not have the aptitude to get into a four-year college. The sad thing was, I believed her. By this time, my father's drinking was getting worse and while he asked me to apply to the four-year college of my choice, I was losing faith in his ability to guide me. I thought the alcohol was distorting his perception and his ability to keep in touch with reality. I really think the white folks began to impact my self-esteem. I was getting worn down, having to repeat pre-calculus twice and Physics twice in my junior year. I was having trouble understanding why my father thought the academic college track was a good thing for me to do.

I enrolled in Queensborough Community College (a two-year college). I took an aptitude test, and the results made the college counselor ask me why I was enrolled there and why I had not applied for a four-year college. I explained my High School counselor's statements and she shook her head. My father's words rang true once again. I had let them beat me down and rob me of my education. I even turned on my father and used his drinking as an excuse to dismiss his advice but here it was in black and white and validated there by testing materials. Not only had I failed myself, but I failed my dad. Wow! This ignited my fire, my determination to prove to white folks that we were equal to them, that I was equal to them, and that I would not be denied my right to be respected as such and to show them by surviving and succeeding in their arenas. My father died in my first semester of junior college. I was angry with him at the time of his death.

In my first year of junior college, I knew it all. My oldest brother turned his back on his four-year college scholarship and returned home to marry his High School sweetheart. My father was sick of him and never connected with his wife because of my brother's marriage to her. My mother could care less one way or the other because her favorite child could do no wrong. Besides quitting college, being married was a big thing for both sides of my family, especially since both my father's siblings and my mother's siblings made a career of being married. Everyone was married and divorce was unheard of; your spouse had to die before you could consider marrying someone else. My aunt, my mother's sister, was the only exception. She had a son she was raising by herself but for the longest time, we never knew where her son came from. I had known real knowledge of sex and babymaking, so my aunt's lifestyle was a mystery to me. It was understood that my cousin was my aunt's son, but his dad was taboo to ask about or discuss. Everyone else knew to stay married and never divorce. My aunt was obviously a rebel but silent about it. If you knew her, you would know that was the only thing she was silent about. She had an opinion about everything, and she wasn't afraid to tell you her opinion. But when it came to divorce, ex-husbands, and children, babies out of wedlock, she was mum, no questions, there was no spoken word ever about it. So, my mother accepted my brother's marriage and my father gave up hope on his oldest son in our house ever being a college graduate. My father was right once again. My oldest brother never went back to college.

My youngest brother graduated from High School without a sports scholarship and enrolled in junior college to avoid going into the service. As I told you early on in the book, my youngest brother always knew what to say or do to make everyone believe he was on top of his business. We went to the same junior college while I was attending class. He was in the cafeteria playing cards, Spades, with his friends. I would stop by and check in between classes. I knew all his friends and they knew me. Even though we were past childhood, the same rules applied to my brother's friends that were told to me as a child, to stay away from my "boys" and for them to stay away from me. As hard as I tried to convince my brother that I could handle it, the stronger he would protest. I finally gave up trying and so did they. But I have got to tell you, some of his friends were so good-looking. The same rule applied to my friends. My brothers were attractive and my friends or so-called girlfriends were always hinting at trying to get with them. My youngest brother and I tried to keep our spoken and unspoken pack against dating our friends. I was more lenient than my brother until he went out with one of my girlfriends. That girl wore me out. Instead of calling to talk to me, she would start out with how are you and what's up but within five minutes or less, the conversation would turn to my brother. At first, I didn't get it. You see, I was trying to set up my argument for dating his friend until the girl just became straight-up annoying. It got to the point that when she called, I would give the phone to my brother as soon as I heard her voice. Needless to say, I was cured of my brother and I dating each other's friends. This girl got so bad with the drama that she removed all thoughts of me ever wanting to date any of my brother's friends. She made my brother and my life miserable. She was clingy, jealous, and a drama queen. When they broke up, she and I salvaged what was left of our friendship. After high school, she became an alcoholic. All she did was talk about high school. I was a senior in college and she had children but all she did was talk about high school.

For two years, I watched my brother and his friends playing cards in the cafeteria and they watched me continue to go to class. Finally, it was the day of graduation and I left.

I had a brand-new determination. I wanted out of my house and away from my mom. I still hated her and now that my father was dead, there was no reason for me to stay. My youngest brother and his friend moved to Atlanta, Georgia. My oldest brother and I had no conversations with each other. He knew the truth and so did I. He and his wife had one baby, my oldest niece. I loved children so I would go spend time with his wife and his daughter. I wanted his wife to be the sister I never had. She was six years older than me and the only girl and the youngest in her family as well. We had some things in common, but the relationship didn't quite work out as I wanted it to. Besides the fact that my father didn't like her, I never could understand why she and I could not get along. To this day, I think she tolerated me and since I hated my oldest brother, it wasn't a problem. After all, I had survived all these years without a sister.

My mom was becoming more and more dependent on me. My oldest brother had no use for my mom until he needed something. My mom was willing to go along with that because she raised him to be who he was. My mom would ask my advice on business dealings and household concerns. I was precocious as a child, and it became very apparent that my mom understood those attributes. I was becoming a crutch. I had not forgotten my mission to prove white folks wrong and my commitment to my father to make it, to graduate from a four-year college, to not be a burden on my husband but to be his support system, and take advantage of every part of the educational system the white man had to offer. So, without my mom's help, I researched and applied to the best local four-year college I could find that would allow me to stay on campus and be within a one-plus hour driving distance from my mother. Even though I hated her, I could not leave her stranded just yet. I had to wean her and myself. I found Stony Brook University. The weather on Long Island in the winter was frost- biting cold just like upstate. New York. Stony Brook was as close to an Ivy League college as I could get that would give me distance from my mom and meet my criterion for staying on campus and not living at home.

COLLEGE YEARS

What an experience my first year of college was. I had to stay off-campus my first semester. Here comes the ugly head of racism again. My time at Bayside High School made me lose my ghetto accent. I was a well-spoken black girl who could be mistaken for white over the phone. Because I blew up my on-campus housing opportunity, I had to find off-campus housing for my incoming semester. I began calling roommate/housemate ads. It was "Yes, we have a place. Why don't you come by and take a look at it?" As soon as my chocolate face showed up, it was oh, we just filled the ad. I would only see the same ad in the paper the following week. And then there was this Jewish family. The husband was a Physics professor on campus, and they had a small child and a beautiful home. Again, it was "Yes, we have a room available. Come by and take a look at it." This time, I had a bit of an attitude once I heard the same words one too many times. This time, I politely said, "I want you to know that I am black so if you do not want to rent to someone of my race, please tell me before I walk to your home from campus." The professor was astonished and appeared to be angry as I was at what had happened to me. He and his wife gave me directions to their home. They were so kind. I ended up staying in their home my first semester. I cried when I finally found on-campus housing because they were like family to me. I had never been exposed to generations of Physicists and a little boy genius. His wife taught me to bake Jewish bread, they invited me to their dinner parties, and they made me feel like family. I learned how to attend small dinner parties and hold intelligent conversations with people who were of a different race and who were of superior intelligence. I was exposed to people who owned beaches on Long Island and who were culturally and economically different from me.

I began hitchhiking to school because sometimes, the professor would give me a ride, but sometimes, he went in early to prepare his lesson plans and I just didn't want to get up. So, I hitchhiked. Yes, the black girl from Jamaica, Queens, hitchhiked. I lived about three miles from campus. It was a good brisk walk but when I was traveling with books and a change of clothes for hanging out with my friends, the walk became overwhelming and tiring sometimes. I would have to take a nap in the library before class just to regain my energy.

One day, I was picked up by a black woman who was an Associate Professor and lived about four blocks from me. She and I became friends. She gave me her number and begged me to stop hitchhiking and to call her when the professor could not take me to school in the morning. She was my first exposure to a black republican. I was in disbelief. I asked her how she could be a Republican in the midst of the Civil Rights movement and affirmative action. After all, the height of the civil rights movement was a little less than ten years prior to our meeting. She explained that her family and her black neighbors, of which there were about ten homes owned by older black Americans in her area, were generations of Republicans and the history behind their political choice. She was a Republican by default. It was so intriguing. My horizons were being expanded and my belief systems were under constant challenge. I soon bought a bicycle and lost touch with her. What an experience. I had to keep looking for on-campus housing because it was hard for me to get to and from the library in the late evenings.

Finally, I was given on-campus housing, so I had to say goodbye to my newfound family. For a while, I continued to check in with the Physics professor just to let him know I was okay and then I soon began to discover campus life. I was consumed with new friends and classes. I lived in the most rinky-dink dorm on campus. I had a roommate who was fast. Boys were her thing and sex was not far behind. She knew all the black guys on campus, and they all seemed to end up in our room. I would pretend to be asleep to avoid the pick-up lines and the party hang-out conversations. I could hear them trying to pick up on me in my pretend sleep, "Look at that ass. If her face looks like that ass, I'm in love." I couldn't wait for the semester to end so that I could get reassigned to a new dorm. Finally, it was over, and I was away from her and her party all- day and night lifestyle. I was approved for and moved to the new dorms on campus, the "suites."

Stony Brook during that time basically had two races, whites and blacks. There were about 17,000 or more students. Less than four percent were black and 90% were white. All the black folks knew each other. I had a home girl that I went to elementary school with that was there and we reconnected and hung out. She established a group of friends with which I became a member. We called ourselves "F" troop after the then-popular army sitcom. At that time, black sororities were rare on lily white campuses, so we had to form our own collective bodies. We didn't have a Sergeant Shultz but we had all the other characters in the show in our click. We hung tough and checked in on each other daily. We exchanged boy stories and all our other problems with trying to survive on a lily-white campus with five hundred people in a lecture hall and teacher assistants that you had to sign up to see and when you finally had your time with them, they were always less than helpful or too white to help a black person that should not be in the same room with them, let alone in the same school. I began having flashbacks to my days at Bayside High School. Their attitudes made me even more determined to beat them at their own game.

I finally moved to my new suite, yes, suite. I was in one of the newest dorms on campus, Roth Quad overlooking a duck pond.

We had three bedrooms in our suite with a connecting living room, bathroom, and a kitchen nook.

There were two girls in each bedroom. The dorm floors were split—boys on one floor and girls on another floor. We had resident assistants that helped to monitor the appropriate dorm behavior as defined in our code of ethics contract that we each signed and promised to obey.

I was happy with my new roommate. She was white but very cool. She had one mission and that was to get through school in four years with a degree. I loved that because my mission was to get a four-year degree as well and I wanted someone who was focused as a roommate instead of a party fly girl like my former roommate. We didn't study together but we would have wonderful social discussions about the world, "society" and where we were going to fit in once we graduated.

My other suitemates and I got along about the same as my roommate and me. There were 6 of us. The other suitemates were insignificant except for this one Jewish girl. She and I looked at each other from a distance and said very little to each other for a long time, almost an entire semester. I spent very little time in my room. I was busy checking in with the "F" troop and following up on some social causes special to my heart. I volunteered and worked at the student hotline for a couple of years. The hotline was the student crisis support center. We helped prevent suicides and incoming freshmen with stress over study/course workloads and being away from home. I remember talking to a person who was so depressed and ready to end his life for hours until we could get our professional parent hospital crisis center on the line to assist me with the call. The hotline wasn't the only thing I had a passion for. There was this smart-alecky brother, a black male, that thought he was Mr. Politician. He ran for school president as a young black man in a sea of white people. I hated his arrogance, but I loved his drive. I immediately connected with his determination to win at the white man's education game and to win big. He campaigned all over the campus. He was tenacious, outspoken, intrusive, and extremely annoying. He would speak about the need to have a general voice to provoke administrative change. He did not run on a black agenda but a common belief system for all students, avoiding color differences. He was brilliant. His father was a politician, and he learned the art of politics well. It was as if he would single me out to have an active debate about campus concerns and my ability to make a difference. He was trying to build a cabinet. We had a full government structure. We had the school-wide president, vice-president, class presidents, and senators representing dorm sections/locations throughout the campus. Stony Brook was a 1,000 acre campus with six sets of dorm areas. Each dorm housed about 200 to 250 students. This brother wanted me in his cabinet. He wore me down. I began campaigning and when election time rolled around, I won unanimously. This was significant because I had white, formidable opponents running against me. I was excited about essentially winning a popularity contest which reflected some trust in my intellectual capacity. It was the first time that my intelligence was validated by my peers, my white peers. I was on a roll.

We had our first student government meeting, and my ego brother was in full form—oh yeah, I forgot to tell you he won, too. He was the final vote on all decisions and if he did not like our vote, he exercised his veto power. He was now a validated arrogant ass. The worst part was because we were both black, it prevented me from openly voicing my disagreement and arguing with him in public. The black students on campus had an unspoken agreement and it was that we would never make each other look bad publicly. We had white folks doing enough of that for us that we weren't going to add fuel to their fire. My newly elected brother would come to my dorm room to secure my vote on certain issues he wanted the senate to pass so that he could avoid continuing to exercise his veto power. We would argue in the dorm, and I would call him everything under and over the sun. However, publicly, I was in his corner. I felt used and betrayed by my political brother. However, his abuse could never outweigh the years of abuse I received at the hands of white folks. I eventually quit and resigned from my position. I told my brother he was on his own. I was tired of being pimped by him under the guise of politics and goodwill.

Between politics, the hotline, and "F" troop, I lost my real mission which was graduating with a great GPA and a degree. My grades took a nosedive. My large science classes with over three hundred students weren't cutting it. I had disappeared into a large deep hole. I was in an academic disaster. Those infamous TAs, the teacher assistants, were like ghosts when it came to digging their heels in to help dig you out of the academic ditches. I was drowning. I would stay up late nights trying to study and memorize my way to better grades. One night, I was up in the suite common area, and I heard my Jewish suitemate's alarm go off. She wakes up and it is 3:00 in the morning. I asked her why she was getting up so early. She replied that she could ask me the same thing. I laughed and said, "I never went to sleep." She decided to respond to my question by saying this is her study time every night except for two nights a week. She woke up at 3:00 AM and studied until about 6:30 AM / 7:00 AM. She had studied our suitemates and determined that these were the quietest hours. I asked her how she could stay awake in class. She said it was easy to take naps during the day. That was the first study tool she gave me. I asked her if she would mind if I joined her if I promised to stay quiet. I explained my grade situation and how I was struggling to turn the grades around. She began to look at my books and my test with me. She was a strong academic student with A/Bs and nothing else, probably more As than Bs. I considered her brilliant because she was taking hard courses and managing to maintain a strong GPA, and grade-point average. She would always say the same thing, that she wasn't brilliant. She attributed her grades to hard work and good study systems. As we went over my grades and study habits together, I began to understand what I was doing wrong. I was studying hard but not smart. The academic work wasn't over my head. I just did not understand how to attack the process and how to design a study approach that would consistently work for my style of learning. We continued to work together in the wee hours of the morning until we graduated. I was initially very, extremely dependent on her to help guide me in discovering what would work for me depending on the subject. She was so gracious and humble. Soon, I was so independent and on track that she would have to ask me to take a break and talk for a moment. My GPA soared. I had to do three and not two years at Stony Brook because of my dismal first year but I kicked ass in the last two years of my stay. I was like my Jewish friend and A/B student. To this day, I am so thankful for my Jewish girlfriend. We stayed in contact our first two years out of school and then we lost touch. I moved from New York to California. If you are reading this book, please call me. I am forever grateful to you.

I lost a lot of my campus friends when I had to do a third year to make up for that first-year fiasco. I was a determined senior without my troop and my former suitemates. I decided to move off the campus again. I met this wonderful professor who had a doctorate in Physiology. I never really understood Physiology, so I decided to take a graduate-level course in the subject to stretch my brain and try on something different. The professor was a six-foot-tall heavy set, blond hair, female from California. She was all the way cool. I had to find a way to get to know her. Her attitudes and her perceptions were so different from the average white New York professor. I did not know if the attitude had to do with the love of Philosophy and the passion behind the love of her field of study. Besides, she was from California, the place I was going to live out my life and I wanted to learn about California from her eyes. Needless to say, we became friends. She lived off-campus in a house that had a room for rent. She and her boyfriend lived there and had one roommate with one available bedroom space for a second roommate. She had a dog and the house allowed dogs. I always wanted my own dog. I made my way to the house. It was big and spacious. The bedroom was larger than the one I shared with my roommates. I was in heaven. I had just bought a car, a little red Fiat. No more bicycles, no more hitchhiking, and no more roommates. I was buying gas now, so I had to find a job. My rent was covered by my student loan. This is the late 70s. I answered an ad for a job babysitting and light housekeeping. I figured how hard it could be to pick up a little girl from school and help clean up a house every day. I was going to be paid seventy-five dollars per week, four days per week, for eight hours of work a week. I was paid a little over nine dollars per hour. I had to pick the little girl up from school, take her to violin & dance lessons, bring her home, and start dinner for the most part. The only problem with the gig was that this was a lesbian couple. In the 70s, free love was alive but lesbians were not cool. Once I met their little girl who was about eight years old, and I realized how sweet she was, so I took the job. It helped to pay for my gas and some groceries since I was living off-campus. I had my meal plan so that I could eat all my meals in the school cafeteria. Sometimes when I arrived home, I wanted a little something to get me through the night.

My Philosophy professor's boyfriend was a mechanic. They shared a room in the house. My Fiat needed brakes on a regular basis. Her boyfriend was from the south with a heavy southern accent. At first glance, he looked and sounded like a true redneck. But he was as sweet as pie. He taught me how to change the brake pads on my car. I wanted to learn anything that saved me money. I was a tightwad and still the same infamous banker as I was known as a kid. I remained true to form as I struggled through my college years. Anyway, on Saturdays, if the weather permitted, my roommate's boyfriend and I were under the car checking out tires and hoses and changing the car fluids. I learned a lot about cars and men while I worked alongside her boyfriend. Her boyfriend was a simple man. He was a white southerner and not complex at all. He knew what he knew and was comfortable with himself. He wasn't a college professor, but he slept with one every night and he remained true to himself. At first, I could not understand how he fits in but then I got it. In order for him to be untouched by her position, he had to be sure of himself. He taught me a lot about cars and a few things about the male species. The two of them taught me a lot about how to select a mate for myself. For them, it wasn't about their egos but about human compatibility.

I learned a lot about the study of and the origin of the study of Philosophy. I also learned about the state of California from my professor's roommate. She was a Californian born and raised. I learned how to speak well with a white well-educated California flair. While at Bayside High School, I was encouraged to use, adapt, and assimilate into white culture in essence and use white speech and language. My roommate helped me lose what was left of my New York accent in trade for my new future life in California. I was prime because I knew I was moving to California after my graduation. I was infatuated with the Golden gate bridge and the ambiance of

Northern California, San Francisco, "Frisco" as we called it on the East Coast. I had never been to Northern California, but I knew this was my new home. I spent a summer in Los Angeles with my childhood friends. I had a ball hanging out with old friends but as a native New Yorker. Los Angeles was too plastic and the people were too self-absorbed with how they looked, the clothes they wore, and who they knew. Even partying was a who's who fashion show. The day social life was worse than the nightlife, all surface level and very superficial. I loved my friends, and if it weren't for them, my summer would have been miserable. Los Angeles was not the place for this Jamaica Queen's girl. But Northern California was different; it was gorgeous. It was like Paris, full of life. I remember thinking, even if the people are assholes, the city made up for it in its landscape, its skyline, and its bridges.

In my next to last year of college, I minored in Education. I began working at an experimental school on campus and interning at an experimental elementary school on Long Island. At the experimental school on campus, I met two new friends. We had a great time at work and began hanging out a lot together off-campus. They had a house they were renting with some other campus students. They were white but really cool. I actually liked hanging out with them. They loved to play the card game "Bridge." I teased them about the game because in my urban world, we played Spades, and Bridge was considered an old white lady's game. There was a disconnect because they were young people meeting in the evenings to hang out and play Bridge. At first, I watched and then I realized the game was a lot like Spades. I played a couple of hands and my urban world snuck into my consciousness. I got up before the whiteness rubbed off on me. Because I liked them and we hung out a lot, I couldn't resist playing a hand or two. Before I knew it, I was hooked. What I did not know about one of my friends is that she was gay. She was white and a gay lesbian. I thought to myself where they are coming from. In my neighborhood, a gay person could not survive. They would be beaten up every day mercilessly. I was so naïve I did not know she was gay. In the late 70s, nobody talked about gay people. It was as if they did not exist. It was considered a sickness. I knew I did not want to catch it, whatever it was. I was so naïve that I agreed to travel with this person still not understanding that she was gay.

A year before I graduated from Stony Brook, I wanted to go to Europe: England, Paris, and France. When I met my friends at the experimental school, they all would sit and talk about their travels in Europe. I had taken the French language from fourth grade through high school. I could read French and my fluency would fade in and out because if I weren't in class, I never used the language. I wanted to travel to Paris because, in the French language books I studied Paris was always showcased. I never liked history or geography, so I didn't know that there were African countries that spoke French. I just knew about what I saw in the language books for so many years. The more my friends talked about their European travels, the more determined I became to go to England and France. I started researching student airfares. I started talking to my friends about taking the trip. They were excited and they wanted to come. We split the research on the trip. I was to find the cheapest airfare. Someone else had bed and breakfast student lodging. Someone had meals, restaurants, and general college student discounts. We were on a roll. As the time for spring break grew nearer, folks started to drop out of the trip. Some did not save up enough money and their parents weren't going to foot the bill. Some had to go to summer school to pull up their GPAs. There were only two people left to travel with. I worked hard. I picked up a few extra jobs and I was good at saving money, especially when I had a mission. My focus and determination were infallible when I wanted something. I could zero in on a task and the blinders would go on for everything other than the target. Once I went into my zone and was clear about my target, I was unstoppable. We both had our money to book the flight and our spending money. We had our friends' research all of our travel accommodations and the best tourist spots, so we were ready to go. There was one glitch. We both wanted to go to England but we split when it came to Paris. She wanted to go to Ireland, and I had to see and experience Paris. So, we went to England together and split up in England and went our separate ways. I was a little nervous being in a place where I knew no one but again, my determination to get to Paris outweighed my fears. I boarded the boat from England and began studying my French. I met a black woman and her son on the boat. She didn't speak French but she was on her way to Paris. I became their tour guide. I was prepared with my maps of hotels and restaurants. I was on my way. Once we reached France, we exchanged our money together for French currency and we took a cab together to the hotel I had researched. When we got there, I helped them get a good price on their room and I got my room and we parted. I was in love with museums, so my first trip was to the museum, Louvre. I loved art and original paintings, Van Gogh's, Rodin's, Picasso's, and the like made me feel like I was in heaven me to heaven. There was one thing I was not prepared for and that was how much French men loved black women. I would just go to sit in the park to watch people and read a book and out of nowhere, there was a French man grabbing my hand, kissing it, and talking to me. At first, I thought it was the location, but it wasn't. I was a French male magnet. It became annoying and unpleasant. Finally, I discovered the Paris student quarter where I met my first African brother from Cameron. He was in love with me, so he said. I was ready to get away from the French men. He took me all around Paris and to Versailles. We rode the train. He was kissing all over me and finding me in public. I had to keep pushing him away. What was so curious to me was how the French people ignored the sexual nature of public displays and when they looked, they just smiled. I was still a virgin and while I considered losing my virginity in Paris, the land of romance and sex, I couldn't because I wanted love. My African brother was great. I went to his apartment. We fooled around but the sex thing was still too much for me. We stayed in touch once I returned to the states. I later discovered from his letters from Cameron that he was royalty. He wanted a wife, but I would have been one of his many wives and I was not ready for that or a move to an African country. We soon lost touch. I kept some of the gifts he gave me for many years until I married my ex-husband.

Finally, on graduation day, my mom, my grandmother, and my aunt and uncle came to my graduation. My brothers couldn't handle my success. I didn't know where they were, and I didn't care. This was my day. My grandmother was so proud of me that she didn't know what to do. She just smiled and smiled some more. After graduation, my housemates prepared dinner for my family. We all sat down at the table and had a wonderful dinner. It was one of the best days of my life. I did it. I proved those white folks wrong, and I did it within their house, their university, and their highly regarded university. I was my grandmother's favorite, and she always told me I could do anything I put my mind to. She knew how much I wanted this, and she lived long enough to see it happen. My grandmother was my confidant, she knew all my secrets, my despair, my silent cries, my pain, and my determination to leave it all behind me. She knew my drive to prove them wrong and my drive to honor my father's dreams. For me, this graduation was for every white person that told me I wasn't good enough or who thought that black people were worthless.

COLLEGE IS OVER;
MOVING ON WITH LIFE

I returned to the states feeling very fulfilled and happy to be in my last year of college. As I prepared for graduation, I also prepared to move to California. I knew I could not return to that 2-bedroom tiny hut I called home. I knew I could not go back to living my life with my mother who I hated but respected enough to take care of anymore. But no way, no, how would I agree to return to those ugly bitter memories? I packed only the things that could fit in my fiat, sold the rest, and went home to prepare to move to California. I created spending money and money to live off in California. I also sold my fiat. I put the California spending money in a cashier's check to avoid spending it prior to leaving New York. My European travel buddy and I decided to travel to San Francisco together. We were both adventurous...

Still, I was oblivious to her gay status until we landed in Denver, Colorado visiting a friend of hers and we headed to a bar party spot. Some of the women there were dressed so much like men that it took me a while to know that they were women and this was a lesbian bar. But before I got wind of it, I was partying and having a good time. After the bar scene, I confronted her and she revealed her status, and we were cool. She never hit on me, and I was cool with that. But I must admit I was a little curious about the lesbian lifestyle but never acted on it. I really loved my brothers and I wasn't willing to give them up for a moment of intrigue. I was tempted by one of her friends, but thank God, nothing happened. The girl was strange yet intriguing, but I wasn't prepared to give up my brothers. The weirdest part of this story was when I arrived in San Francisco. I did not know anyone and my friend had a sister friend who was gay and lived in San Francisco. She had a live-in lesbian partner. I stayed in her friend's one-bedroom plus loft apartment with her and her partner for a few weeks while I located a white friend's family that lived in Novato, California. At this point, I needed another option. I was caught in a world I was not used to and I had no desire to stay in.

The family I got in contact with was white, husband and wife with two children. They said I could stay with them until I found a job and my own place. I slept on their couch. Again, I was in a lily-white neighborhood going to their private tennis club for entertainment, babysitting while the wife played tennis and again subject to the general steering by all the uppity white folks who wanted to know who let me in. But my new friends were powerful and held to the fact that they paid dues and there were no rules or signs saying no blacks allowed. I just could not get away from racism.

While I liked the lesbian couple, I was cramping their style and they were cramping my sense of morality. We parted on good terms. Sometimes when I was stranded in San Francisco late at night, I would call her and stay over. Novato was at least a thirty-minute bus ride from San Francisco. Soon, I found a studio apartment and I got a job teaching at a private school in San Francisco. I was ready to move. I ran into the biggest racist and economic problem with a well-known conventional popular bank. Then, the banks were not national but state-governed and ruled. I put a cashier's check for five thousand dollars plus in this bank from another well-known bank in New York and it took approximately two months for the cashier check to clear. While I had pocket money, I was counting on that money to pay the deposit on my apartment and to get some things I needed until I found a job. It did not quite work out like that. I had to work with what I had in hand, and I had to get a job. Again, I did not realize my status in the world. I thought I was in a gay city full of people of color and all cultures and how could they see a young black girl as a problem? I had a cashier's check from the New York bank I understood that inter or intra-state banking was not yet in place but when months went by without access to my funds, I began to understand that this was more than just holding a check. I realized that racism was alive in San Francisco, California. Wow, the difference for me was that in New York, if folks didn't like you for whatever reason, it was clear up front, no game-playing, no smiling in your face. It was clear and while they did not call you a nigger to your face, they made sure you understood it wasn't happening. Whatever you wanted, weather it was a job, a bank account, or a place to live once you stepped into the place, you knew walking out of the place wasn't going to be. In California, people were always so friendly and so inquisitive. I would stand at a bus stop and people would start talking to me as if I had known them for a while. I would look at them in a very curious mode trying to understand what gave them the authority or permission to invade my space without asking. It didn't happen just at the bus stop as it was common practice. As time went on, I concluded that California has a superficial, very surface-level social convention, which was true for the bus stop and the corporate office. All smiles, healthy handshakes, patterned answers, great smiles, and well-developed personal somewhat intruding discussions, always left me feeling like I had just made a friend but not so. It was more like a false prevoto. It reminds me of old folks' saying that "All that glitters is not gold." I discovered that Californians had a very pretentious way of existing. I didn't learn about this part of California from my Philosophy professor. She conveniently left out a discussion about Californian culture.

I ended up staying in Novato long enough to find my first teaching job in San Francisco and a second job, a part-time job, in the evenings. My first paychecks covered my deposit on my apartment. I met some really great landlords who held my studio apartment for almost three months while I waited on Bank of America to release the check. Finally, that was no longer my issue because I had two jobs. I wish I could have sued Bank of America, but I was young and naïve. I had gotten so used to white folks treating me like a second-class citizen that this was just another incident that fueled my fire. By the time I discovered the inconsistencies in the banking laws and how I was treated, the statute of limitation for a lawsuit against them had passed.

Besides, I had moved around so much that I no longer had my copy of the original cashier's check or the supporting documentation. I was still very young and dumb.

My apartment was about three blocks from the lesbian couple I stayed with when I arrived in San Francisco. I kept in touch with them because they were the only people I knew in San Francisco. The friend I traveled from New York with always had friends that were into all kinds of socially positive things. Her friend in San Francisco was conducting counseling groups for gay, lesbian, and questioning young women. I think the young people were fifteen to twenty years old. She wanted some help. She wanted me to use my degree in Psychology to help her with the co-facilitation of the group. At that time, I was taking University of Berkeley Psychology graduate level classes through their extension program. I was working on trying to get an internship with the Psychology professors. Working with the group was consistent with my aspirations to become a psychologist. It was weird at first but because I was so open-minded, I was able to make a shift in my thinking from young people trying to decide to be gay to young people trying to find and define themselves sexually. The problem was their sexuality wasn't the real issue. The real issues were their relationships with their families. Woo, that was deep and hard to keep them focused on because they were hiding behind their sexual choices. They were some street-wise, tough, hardcore young women. I stayed with the group for a while until work and the need for more money took over. The counseling gig was volunteer work.

NEW JOBS, NEW EXPERIENCES, NEW PEOPLE IN MY LIFE

I moved into my studio apartment. I landed a teaching job. The Berkeley atmosphere on campus and surrounding the campus was more than I could handle. The people were a major distraction, odd, left-thinking, and straight out of the Haight Ashbury psychedelic movies but transplanted into everyday people and everyday living. Everything that could be thought of to do that was weird and off-base occurred in Berkeley and on the campus. Even the graduate psychology professors had adapted to the environment and were sporting the oddball culture that fit in the Berkeley culture. I was born and raised in New York. I was conservative, liberal, and I thought somewhat open-minded. Even with all my exposure, I was in no way prepared for the Berkeley lifestyle which had infiltrated the campus. I quickly rethought my dedication to the field of Psychology. I traded in my dreams of becoming a psychologist for becoming an educator. I always loved teaching and young people.

I met a new friend at the bus stop. We were always running out of our apartments at the same time to catch the same bus. We began to laugh and talk because the bus driver knew our morning schedules and would hold the bus for both of us. I began to look for her as I was walking in the morning to the bus stop and her for me. We would laugh as we did the OJ Simpson commercial morning run to the bus stop. We began to talk and realized how much we had in common. We were neighbors for six-plus years. We knew each other's families. I would go to major holiday dinners at her family's house. She had a large family and her mom and dad always had dinner ready for extra friends of the family.

My bus stop friend and I were hangout buddies. We went to socially conscious and religious events, and we partied together. We were groupies with our reggae brothers. We went backstage and to their hotel rooms. We were in love with the reggae beat and the reggae brothers. Both of us had a real bohemian flavor, and the reggae brothers loved it. My girlfriend dated the lead singer and writer of a famous reggae group. I just hung out with one of the band members, nothing too tough, but it kept me occupied. I was never into sex without love.

I was living and working in San Francisco, now the place I had dreamed about. Again, my dreams and my goals were realized. I loved San Francisco. No matter where you go in the city, there is a view. Every location in San Francisco has a hill from the richest to the poorest communities and the views from the hills are amazing. Walking in the city gave me plenty of exercises. I lived in San Francisco ten months out of the year. That is one of the reasons why I enjoyed teaching. Teaching gave me an automatic two-month vacation once a year. I worked ten months, and I was off for two. My part-time job meant that I left in July and returned in September. I lived in New York for the other two months. I banked and saved enough money to make my two-month New York stay possible. I had no real expenses because I stayed at my mother's house. While there, I helped my mother catch up on her personal finance and business concerns. My oldest brother lived about twenty blocks from my mother but only saw her when it was convenient for him and his family. My youngest brother moved from Georgia to San Diego, California, where he got married and had an instant family of two children. My mother was literally in New York without her children's support. While I still had strong feelings of hatred toward my mom, I was raised to be a very God-conscious person. Turning my back on my mother was like turning my back on God. I took solace in the fact that I had a great distance between us, and I knew my time was limited and I could do my part and leave.

While living in San Francisco and feeling good about conquering another goal, I realized I needed a new goal. I wanted to go to law school. I was determined to fulfill another one of my father's goals for me. First was graduating from their colleges and getting their degrees, meaning white folks. His second goal for me was for me to become a lawyer. I decided to prepare for the entrance exams into law school. I took some exam preparation classes. I took the exams and now it was time to apply for schools. I couldn't decide whether I wanted to be on the East Coast or the West Coast. While in New York, I explored going to Columbia University in Harlem. Before, I left my bus stop friend and I had talked about law schools in the Bay Area. Her sister was performing at Hastings law school and my buddy met this African-American law student who was trying to actively recruit more black folks into their school. She couldn't wait for me to return to the West Coast to meet him. She was on a mission to keep me in the Bay Area. As soon as I landed in San Francisco, she had me come straight to Hastings for their black history performance. She promised to give me a ride home. When I walked in, there was this guy standing at the door. He opened the door with a wonderful smile, and he greeted me. I saw my buddy across the room and went over to sit with her. She turned to introduce me to the gentleman who could help me get into law school and it was the guy with the smile. He later became my husband and my ex-husband.

THE GUYS

After our first meeting at the law school, we exchanged numbers, and I did not hear from him for a while. While in New York, the summer before I met him, I began to rethink my going to law school. I was becoming a career student. I was taking graduate classes in Psychology at UC Berkeley. I thought psychology, child development with an emphasis on testing instruments, was my lifelong journey. I spent some time in Berkeley and I was overwhelmed by the eclectic behavior and the strange lifestyles. People were walking around nude on and off campus. Internships with professors were referenced by my own psychosis and ability to recognize them. I was asked questions about whether or not I was neurotic or if I had any stress-related psychosis. I wanted to know what that had to do with wanting a research internship with a psychology professor. Those questions along with the very strange behavior of the Berkeley students and residents made me leery of doing anything in the field of psychology. I decided that I needed to table my pursuit of a graduate degree in psychology. I was straight out of New York, probably at that time, one of the largest conservative urban cities in America. I wasn't ready for crazy. I gracefully bowed out and went back to teaching full-time. Money started getting crazy, so I took on a second job in addition to teaching during the day.

I met a new boyfriend while waiting for my law school guy to call. We met at one of my girlfriends' and my social conscious events. She and I were always at some black cause, promotion, or artistic event. We were true bohemian pan-African sisters. We loved brothers and we were down with anything that promoted or advanced our people. Of course, we had to get a little partying as well. We loved all kinds of black music. We would go to jazz, rhythm and blues, or reggae clubs depending on our mood.

I met my new boyfriend at a black art and poetry reading event. He was very entrepreneurial and had his own business and was really into making money. He asked me the hard question of how long I would continue to work two jobs to support myself. He asked me why I did not just move and get a roommate to cut down on my expenses. I was clear that I did not want to live with anyone else. I had my share of housemates and roommates in college. I was prepared to work three jobs if it meant that I could come home to my own place and have known one there but me, myself, and I. So, he asked that I consider changing careers. I thought about it for a moment and then I began pursuing different career paths. I was always a strong math student, and I loved math. I decided to follow my passion for math and finance. I went back to school to study computer engineering. After my technical development, I landed a job in the computer hub of Northern California, Silicon Valley. I quit teaching and my part-time job and began work as a Software Engineer. I programmed computers and developed software for a hard drive backup system company. I provided quality control and traveled as a system support person for the firm. I tripled my income. I was making three times more than both the teaching and the part-time job put together. My boyfriend was an angel in disguise. I was able to buy a car and I was shopping at Saks 5th Avenue, Nordstrom & Macy's professional wear and designer clothes department. I was back to my shoe fad. Only I wasn't buying flats but designer pumps in all colors and styles. I couldn't travel to the East Coast as much anymore but when I had business trips on the East Coast, I would stop and see my mom. There was one problem: I lived in San Francisco and commuted about thirty minutes on a good traffic day; an hour and a half on a bad traffic day to work every day. Traffic wasn't bad if I left early in the morning and came home late at night. I was actually pretty consistent with my workaholic business schedule. After totaling one car in an accident and about three years of commuting, I grew tired. The commute was taking its toll on me.

About four years into the commute, the company I worked for began having financial problems. They began laying people off. Eventually, we received the sad news that they were going out of business. We received our severance pay and they dissolved the corporation.

Finally, the guy from Hastings started calling. I wasn't interested in talking to him anymore because I had already made up my mind about not going to law school. I already explained my position to him. He was persistent and said we should still talk. I was willing to talk but I told him I did not think he could persuade me at that point. I shared with him that I was tired of school, and I wanted to settle down and have a family. I did not want to become a career student. We set a date to meet. I gave him my address and told him to come over. As soon as I hung up the phone, I thought to myself, what am I doing? I did not know this guy. He could be a serial killer. I immediately tried to call him back to cancel the date. There was no answer for a few days and then one day before the meeting, I called all my girlfriends and told them to call me every ten minutes while he was there to make sure I was okay. I gave them all the details about him as much as I had to give. I was freaked out. Soon, the doorbell rang. I looked. It was him. I saw that big smile again. He was on time. We sat in my apartment and talked for a while but as you can guess, my girlfriends were on it and they called every ten minutes like clockwork. It got so bad we left the apartment and went to the park in my neighborhood. It was a beautiful day in San Francisco and the park was full of people hanging out. We talked so effortlessly. Before I knew it, a couple of hours had gone by, and I had not noticed the time. We walked back to my apartment. I said goodbye and he kissed me on the cheek. I knew then something was going on more than an application and admittance to Hastings Law School.

I received another phone call under the guise of my law school application, and I politely said I wasn't interested. The next call was for a date. After about three years of dating, we were married. In the dating phase, there were some real issues. We worked through them. He had two children from a previous marriage. They were then three and five years old. Today, they are twenty-eight and thirty-one. Yes, a lot of time has passed. Anyway, they were great children. I was a child lover. I thought I had a market in child-rearing with a degree in child psychology and a minor in education I knew I could handle children. Little did I know that there was a real difference between practical vs. application, as I quickly learned. After we got through our three years of struggle as a couple, we grew closer and closer. We broke up after about six months. I was determined to leave him, and I started dating other people. My housemate had something else in mind. She decided that she wanted to play matchmaker. While she hated my status in life, she was convinced we belonged together.

My ex-husband and I tried shacking up for about a year. He had more women friends than male friends. I was cool with it until this one sister wanted to call anytime and he found it necessary to excuse himself from the room while he talked with her. My antennas went up and I began to snoop to figure out the extent of the relationship. I was not down with being disrespected in a house that my man and I shared. I missed a period, and my periods were always like clockwork with no cramps and no pains. I had to write my cycles on the calendar to stay on top of them. If not, they would just appear and that was not good. I took a home pregnancy test and I told him about the baby, and he went there. He suggested that it could be someone else's and the war was on. My monogamy and my pride were worth more than the relationship. I wasn't down for mistreatment or disrespect. I had no real affiliation with a church and even if I did, I felt like God could not want me to bring a child into a world that the parents would not love. So, I made my appointment at the abortion clinic. I was through with it all. What was I going to do now because I gave up my apartment and all my things were in the place we shared? I was a woman of principle and I was never going to be with someone who disrespected me or who thought I was something I wasn't. I was never a sleep-around girl and I resented being pegged as one. My ego kicked in and I was through with the relationship and with him. He traveled a lot for his job. I forgot to mention that while we were together in those three years of dating, he graduated from law school.

He started working for the national law association and he traveled a lot. This time when he went out of town, I drove him to the airport like I always did, and he said he would see me in a few days. I said okay, but I had different plans. He left his itinerary as usual. As soon as I dropped him off at the airport, I called my Ethiopian girlfriend that had a house with a spare bedroom and asked her if she was interested in having a roommate. She said yes and it was a done deal. That weekend, I packed up all my stuff: mattresses, couches, rugs, sheets, clothes, etc. And moved from Oakland back to my stomping grounds in San Francisco. During my move, I came across a letter from the woman who was calling at all times and it went something like this, "Hey, honey, you know I can't wait to get with you. I am longing for your touch. I spend sleepless nights thinking about the time when we can be together." My suspicions were confirmed. If I learned nothing else from that experience, it was that the truth will always reveal itself you don't have to do much as my grandmother said and mother always says, "What you do in the dark will always show in the light sooner or later but don't fret. It will show." I picked him up from the airport as usual and drove him home. He asked me after he got out of the car if I was coming in and I said with the biggest smile, "No, I don't live here anymore." I was done, though, and had no need to even talk about it. I went on with my life and began dating.

MY HOUSEMATE

I also had a good buddy from Ethiopia who I met at another job. She was the exact opposite of me. She was the supervisor at my part-time evening job. She and I became housemates after I left, then my boyfriend who later became my husband and now my ex-husband. She was different; she had a thick accent and was dating only men with money. She thought if the man I was with did not have a deep pocket bank account, then I should leave him alone. She was from royalty, and she expected nothing less than money in her life. I, on the other hand, was searching for love. I wanted a man who loved me, and I wanted to give that love in return. My philosophy was that if he had a vision, the money would come. She didn't like my ex-husband at all at first. She thought he was beneath me. Even though I wasn't from royalty, she felt like I deserved the world and should act like that and expect no less. She made me feel like men should bow at my feet.

Her father came from Ethiopia where he was exiled as a part of the government overthrow. He was exiled to a land parcel he owned in Ethiopia. He no longer held a position of power and respect. He spoke no English, but he spoke their native tongue and French. I spoke French but it was broken because even though I had studied the language since elementary school and through college, I never used it in my everyday life. He and I would be alone in the house, and we would begin to communicate. He with a little English and a lot of French and me with a little French and a lot of English. We were on a roll; we communicated through a little sign language here and there and we managed to form a friendly bond.

My Ethiopian roommate and I were exact opposites, but we shared a heart of gold and a need to always uplift the underdog. We were like Yin and Yang but we met in the middle. During our time together, she dated two men at the same time. They both had money or the look of money. She loved high-power men, movers, and shakers and she commanded them the way they commanded their business or their profession. I became friends with one because she was set on having us date before she began dating him. I wasn't interested in him as a boyfriend but there was something about him that always intrigued me. He was a lawyer and a businessman. He had a sharp mind and perhaps, I was intrigued by his intellect.

My Ethiopian housemate met my ex-husband at a few events and really liked him. They hit it off. He would call the house asking for me and I would say a few words and ask him not to call anymore. Soon, I stopped taking his calls. My housemate on the other hand enjoyed talking to him. I would come in from work or a party and they would be talking. I would go to bed and move on with my life. He worked with her and she worked with me. I finally agreed to meet and talk with him to get him off my back. He apologized and talked a lot. I was worn down by the apologies, explanations, and genuine expressions of love. We were married less than one year after we got back together.

After I got married and moved out of the home my roommate and I shared, he and I ended up in the same city and we ran into each other from time to time. My Ethiopian roommate and I lost touch after I married. I think it was because while she liked my ex-husband's charm, she didn't like his economic status. He was in her words "beneath me." I saw her once or twice in the past ten years. I introduced her to my children but somehow, our friendship wasn't the same.

I have passed through so many people who were my friends in different periods of my life. Each one of them has taught me something great about myself and each one has exposed me in different ways to the world. My sadness happens when I cannot seem to be able to keep them as close friends as I continue my journey through life. All of them have been my guardian angels because, without them, I would not have the rich experiences in my life that sends chills and tears through me as I go back in time to bring their memories present. They are all a part of my every fiber of life.

BECOMING A MUSLIM

I became a Sunni Muslim at the same timeframe as my marriage. I studied Islam for about two years. After gaining a clear understanding of the religion, I took my Shahadah—my commitment to follow the Islamic religion. My ex-husband introduced me to Islam. I followed the Nation of Islam in New York including the five percenters and ten percenters. I knew enough about the nation of Islam to tell me I wasn't interested in their religion. I loved some of their principles. I totally disliked their treatment of women. Our brothers look sharp in the nation in those suites and bow ties, but it looked like the broker's entire being was caught up in the religion.

When I was introduced to Sunni Islam, it was like I was in church. It wasn't about religion. It was about a way of life and a special relationship with God. I no longer needed a mediator or an interpreter. I could talk to God myself through the devotion of my five prayers a day and the study of the Quran. My study of the religion revealed the truth of where women fit in the religion. The level of respect for women was overwhelming. Prophet Mohammed (peace be upon) brought freedom for female children to be born and for their birth to be public and not hidden for fear of having them killed. He married more than one wife to eliminate the starvation of divorced and widowed women. All of this is in the history of the life of Prophet Mohammed. I was blown away by the perceptions given to us by Islamic countries and their treatment of women and by the Nation of Islam and its treatment of women.

You are so afraid of their feelings. You don't want them to remove the high place, the pedestal, that they have you on. You are to them a single Muslim mom who doesn't need the love of a man to survive. So, for that reason, you don't ask or demand full disclosure of your relationship to the world.

Your public self loves the idea of living within the mandates of Islam. It's safe. Being the perfect woman who does not bring a man into her bed in front of her children is correct and therefore the relationship is no one's business but yours and his. Your public self wants and requires the marriage, the wedding, and the ring to feel right about you and to be accepted by the world. Inside your heart, both your public and private self just want the love and affection of a man, your man. Both selves want to be truthful with family, friends, and the world in general but in order for this to happen, you have to decide to stop battling between both selves. You have to decide whether your image is more important than your heart. You have to break the stereotypes and images you have set up with your family, friends, religious community, and former co-workers. You have to take a risk. Your private self loves just being with your boyfriend and discovering new ways to be in a loving relationship with a man. Let go of your fears about your children's reaction to a man that is so different from their dad. Forget about your fears of being challenged by friends who know you and may say that he is not good enough for you. Release your fear of your boyfriend not being able to handle public scrutiny. You have met his family. The truth is you don't know if you are strong enough to be placed under the public microscope yet another time. You know that your kids have gone thru a lot with your divorce from their father. You are not sure if you want to introduce another relationship with a man yet. Take a risk! Stop living behind the door. It's alright to be wrong but being safe is boring. Reach for the stars and if you don't make it, keep trying and reaching. Your past was painful, but you get to define your future. Reach for your happiness with no regrets. Learn from the past and keep pushing *thru. You are worth it and if he is worth anything and the relationship is powerful enough, great things will happen. If not, keep taking risks, until you find that powerful exciting love but don't hide and don't be ashamed. The past is over. It's your life—live it!*

I Love You,

Your Private & Public Self

Becoming a Muslim

I continued my study of Sunni Islam for years. I attended prayer classes and Sunday history classes. I talked with befriended African and African American Sunni Muslim brothers who knew the religion like they knew their life history. I was intrigued by the fact that my place of worship was full of African Americans who could speak Arabic like it was their native tongue. I was intrigued by their enthusiasm and their love of Islam.

My prayer teacher was a tall dark-skinned African-American Muslim brother with a smile that could light up New York City. He had a heart that could do the same. I would stay after class to ask questions about my fears and my mistrust of my interpretation of what I had read or heard. He would always caution me not to listen to others but instead read them for myself. I never could get with the Arabian sister dress, called hijab in the religion. I was a businesswoman working in Silicon Valley. I was not going to wrap my hair and my body like an imitation Arab. I pulled my prayer teacher and brother to the side, and I would say, "Brother, I am really starting to love this religion, but I am not one to cover my head." I told him I could dress modestly because that is the way I have dressed all my life. However, that Arab drapery for a wardrobe was not my thing. He would say, "Sister, you don't have to dress like an Arab to be a Muslim. You just have to be modest and as far as your hair covers, well you are just going to be bald in the hereafter." I looked at him and he would start smiling and we would both break out in laughter. He was well-versed and extremely knowledgeable of Islam. "Thank you, brother man, may you rest well in the hereafter."

My ex-husband was jealous of my prayer teacher. Looking back, I could see how close my prayer teacher and I were. We were friends. My ex-husband thought that he was the only one responsible for teaching me the religion. He would chastise me for turning to other brothers for direction in the religion because he would state that Islam says, "A husband is a wife's first teacher."

After I made my formal acceptance of the religion, I left my prayer brother and began to ask my ex-husband the questions I would have asked my prayer brother. It was hard because my ex-husband did not have the same flare, knowledge level, or experience with working with new Muslims. It was a disaster; I was frustrated with my ex-husband's ego and jealousy. So, I started seeking out very knowledgeable women in the religion. I met my business partner with the school in our Muslim community. She was perfect for me. I watched her for a while in the masjid, our church. She wore modest clothes, not that Arab garb, and every once and a while, she would throw on a regular hat to cover her hair. She would wear scarves in all kinds of styles. The brothers and the sisters in the masjid respected her. She helped to introduce music into our community. She wrote Muslim songs that were centered in a new style of Islamic music. This was new to our Islamic community but very much a part of our African-American Muslim culture. She and her group sang at our wedding. It was crazy because prior to our wedding, I don't think many people danced at a Muslim wedding in our masjid. People looked stiff and confused as if they traded their African-American culture for a straight jacket. My ex-husband and I broke the ice. We started dancing and I could see my sister's partner smiling as she sang. We were kindred spirits.

She was a musician, songwriter, author, and literary scholar when it came to Islam. *"Even as a Muslim woman I feared my unmarried relationship after my divorce. I was afraid of the perceptions that my muslim sisters and brothers may have."* I was honored by her presence. She was down to earth and a regular person. After I got over her fame and mysticism, I was able to be me. We genuinely liked each other and became friends. She was my new resource. I could avoid my ex-husband's jealousy and I began to learn more and more about the religion I was falling in love with, Islam. I was like a sponge, I couldn't get enough information about the religion, and I began buying more and more resource guides. I began focusing my study on women in Islam. My Muslim sister friend invited me to a study group with women and for Muslim women. I met some heavy-hitter Muslim sisters that were fluent in Arabic and wanted, like me, to learn more about Islam. I was over my head when it came to speaking and reading Arabic. Their struggles were deeper and far different from mine. I was trying to figure out how to pronounce an Arabic letter. They were perfecting their fluency in the Arabic language. They were patient with me, and my sister partner and I agreed to meet one weekend day a week to help me build my Arabic skills. Surprisingly enough, my ex-husband watched the kids and had nothing to say when I went out in the evenings to my sister-to-sister Muslim study group meetings.

My Arabic classes with my sister's partner on the weekends started out well, but instead of just my learning Arabic, we began talking about so many other things. Our friendship became stronger than ever. We would discuss our equal passion for education and the problems we had with the schools that were supposed to be educating our children, but instead, we were creating obstacles to their learning. Hence, the birth of our school was in response to our dissatisfaction.

We soon discovered our love and passion for achieving the impossible. We checked in with our husbands and got their approvals to begin work on our very own school. We were on a mission. After we birthed the school, in addition to co-directing the school, my partner wrote a book on women in Islam and put a dedication in the book to me. I was so honored and inspired. I am still my sister. I pray Allah has a special place in paradise for her.

MY MARRIAGE

The day after we got married, my husband's ex-wife sent her two beautiful kids to live with us, and they never left. I had an instant family, a daughter, and a son. My daughter was younger than her brother. I asked them what they wanted to call me, and they left and talked to each other for a moment and came back and decided they would call me mom. There was instant love between us. Our feelings were mutual. I loved them and they loved me. We had a tiny two-plus bedroom apartment. My husband's brother and our two children ended up living with us. I lost my job when the company in Silicon Valley went bankrupt. I took some of their clients and started my own business. I was working with small, medium, and large businesses setting up and designing software and hardware. Soon after, my husband lost his job and he started his own business, acting as a paralegal, writing wills, setting up business plans, and more. We were barely making it. I was getting clients and building my business for about two years before I got pregnant. I had a difficult pregnancy, so I had to drop off clients to take care of myself. We were all excited, my husband and our two children, from his first marriage. We wanted to have six children. We had two and we were on our way. Needless to say, I lost a lot of business during those tough times during the pregnancy. I tried to hire someone, but that old adage is true, "No one treats your business like you do." Well, the employees were flaky and inconsistent, and it made matters worse. I decided to just shut down until after the pregnancy. I started back once the baby was born. I would bring the baby along with me and breastfeed while working. I did that until she was old enough to go to preschool. When she turned two, I found a wonderful preschool and I was back to my business full-time. My husband was in and out of jobs but with each new job, he made more money. I was always making more money than him and hustling my butt off. I was no stranger to hard work; I was used to working for what I wanted or felt I needed. My family's welfare was my primary concern. Besides, my dad said, "There may be a day when your husband can't take care of his family. You get your education in case that day arises when you have to take care of your family on your own." I took his words to heart, and I was prepared to make a comfortable life for my children. True to form, I went after everything I wanted. I was like a piranha. Once I found the bait, I was going to attack and make it mine. I was and still am a taskmaster. Once the task was defined, I was going to achieve it. I was and still am very creative and innovative. I could figure out formulas for meeting the objective and implement them. I got tired of my small contracts that were paying small money, so I set out to find larger clients. As I began my networking, I went after a large government client. The problem was the client would not offer me the contract but instead wanted to hire me. They offered me more than my net business income and health and retirement benefits. At that time, my husband was not making more than their proposal and he was in business for himself as well. We had a growing family with no health benefits. So, after careful consideration and joint conversations with my husband, I took the offer. I shut down my business because I could not raise 3 children, work a full-time job, and run a business. I was a superwoman, but this was outside of reality for her.

After a year, I began to seek jobs with higher pay within the organization. I was grateful for the position, but I knew I could do better. True to form, I set my sites on a higher position which could double my pay and add a little more challenge. I went for it. I got the position, and I was again making more money than my husband. It didn't matter to me because I was following my father's words. I thought it didn't matter to my husband because, at home, I was the traditional wife. I took care of the kids, cooked the food, cleaned the house, and performed my wifely duties on demand. I was the boss from nine to five and the mother and wife after five and on weekends. My husband thought I was competing with him. He never understood that I was my competition. I set goals for myself, and I achieved them for myself. I had an inner drive that transcended marriage and children. The drive was what defined me, not the individual competition around me, including him. My husband would make challenging statements to me that took me outside of being a wife and a mother and put me in my head with my own competitor, myself. He thought those statements would discourage me but instead, they encouraged me to take on more and still work at being the best mom and wife. I was very mechanical about my life. I had formulas for being the best wife, mother, and businesswoman. Two years into my new position, it was time for us to expand our family. We wanted six children, and at this point, we had three. I had my next child. This time, my aunt came to live with us after the baby was born. She was a live-in nanny for my secondborn and helped take care of the other three children. After I had my second daughter, I breastfed her and went back to work. I pumped my milk during the day. I used my breaks and lunches to pump my daughter's milk. I was still the boss at work and the mom and wife at home. My husband found a job and he was now a boss too. I was still making more money than him, but he had less time at home. He began traveling again but I was still the full-time mom and wife. Sometimes, the kids and I would travel with him and share his hotel space. The children really enjoyed that. Then something happened with my job, and I came into a large sum of money. My position was reevaluated and reclassified. It turned out I was being underpaid and I was given retroactive pay for the years this took place. I also received a pay increase. I decided that I would not cash that check but that we should use the money to buy a house. My husband and I disagreed. He thought we should pay off bills that we were successfully paying off with our current budget plan. I refused to use the money for that purpose because we were on track with our bill payments. Our family needed more, and I wanted more for our family. I wanted to purchase a home. He thought I was just talking. I had a friend in real estate, and I told her what I was looking for and she began to find properties for me. I would invite my husband to come along to see the properties. He came to see some of them and made some comments. The real estate person found something in our price range and the owner only wanted to sell it to another black family. My husband came by to see the house. He had some comments and left. I asked the real estate agent to begin talking to the seller. I would give my husband updates about what was happening with the negotiations. One night in bed, he told me he did not want to buy a house right now. I explained that we needed to buy a house, we had four children, and we needed more financial security. He said no. That night, we agreed that if I bought the house, he would leave me. I said okay. One week later, the real estate person brought me the keys to the house and said it was mine. I qualified for the house on my own by lying and stating that I was a single woman, without my husband's credit or any financial support from my husband. The house was in my name and two weeks later, I took everything that was in our rental home that belonged to me including my two oldest children and my two youngest children and moved to my house. My husband left me after six years of marriage and three years of dating prior to our marriage.

I was so happy in my new home. My aunt, my mother's sister, was my nanny and she stayed with me so that I could continue to work, pay my house note, and take care of my children. Again, I knew instinctively that this was the right thing to do and that I would probably not have this opportunity again in my lifetime. I owned my first home, a five-bedroom, two-bathroom home. My heart was broken but my head was in the right place.

After a little over a year went by, my two oldest children went between their dad and me to live. It was awkward, but we made it through. Soon, the phone calls started from my soon-to-be ex-husband. He had a softer voice, a smoother sound, and slowly, we began to reconsider our separation. We started dating again and before we knew it, he had moved into my house. This was a mutual decision. I always wanted what was best for my family. I believed that both parents living together and raising their children was the best thing for a family. I never had any pretenses around my thoughts about family.

Family to me was second only to God-consciousness. I believe that the black family is the cornerstone of our culture and our heritage. I wanted to have all of my children by the same man, and I wanted to be married to that man before I started having children. This was a principle in my life that I dedicated my way of life to and my existence. So, I did what was necessary to keep my family together.

I had two children in high school and two children in elementary school. The schools they were attending did not meet my standards for their education. It was too late for me to do something about my high school children, but I could create some prevention for the younger set. So, the birth of my second business was in the making. I had a very well-educated girlfriend who had recently adopted three children. Two of the children were her nieces who she had to take away from a family member. One child was the product of a formal adoption process that she and her husband had begun before they learned about her two nieces. They were looking for one child and they ended up with three. She was an extremely talented sister, a strong Muslim, a writer, a singer, and an educator. She was my Muslim sister. She helped me learn more about my religion, Islam. She had a special love and appreciation for the beauty of Islam. I went to Muslim women's study groups with her, and she began teaching me the language of the Quran, Arabic. We would meet on Saturday mornings for her to teach me the Arabic language. Sometimes, those Saturdays were spent chatting about our passion for educating our children instead of my learning the language. We would laugh about my avoidance and intimidation of the Arabic language. I would always find some way to distract us from the task at hand. My best distraction was a discussion on our unhappiness with the schools in the area. After we vented, we would begin to talk about what we felt a perfect school would look like.

About two years later, my third child was born, a boy. We now had five of the six children we talked about at the beginning of our relationship, but we both agreed that number five was enough. Our son was a welcomed surprise. He was not planned but definitely wanted. We were having some relationship problems, but our son was a special part of both of our hearts. My entrepreneurial spirit kicked in again. I was not happy with my children's education, and I was not willing to continue to ignore my dissatisfaction. I knew we couldn't afford the quality I was looking for and even if we could, I wanted more than what was available in the Oakland marketplace.

My ex-husband thought the Muslim school was the answer and the solution to our children's education. I abided by his wishes for the first two children and when our third child was born, I ventured out a little. The Muslim school would not take our youngest daughter until she was two and a half, but I needed to leave my business and take a nine-to-five job. So, I found a great African-American school owned by an African-American family and catered to African-American children. Notice I moved from "black" to "African-American." Times were changing. We were moving into the 90s. My daughter went to the school until she completed kindergarten then my ex-husband convinced me it was time for her to learn our religion. We put her in the Muslim school but the workload was too easy in the first grade. So, we had her tested and moved to the second grade. A big mistake in retrospect, she was very mature, but she missed some basic skills that should have been given to her in the first grade and the same skills were not covered in the second grade. Even with that, she was still testing well scholastically. My daughter began to outgrow their academic curriculum and I was not satisfied. So, I moved her back to the African-American school for one year. This one year was the planning year for our new school. My Muslim sister friend and I had moved from the talking phase of sharing our miseries to laying the framework for our own school.

THE CREATION OF A SCHOOL

We chatted every other night and met every Saturday or Sunday until we had the business plan and mapping for our school. We shared a mutual passion as educators to teach our own children and others. We knew we had a winning formula. I talked to my ex-husband who was critical of our vision, and she spoke to her husband. We wanted their okay before we committed our souls to our passion. I don't think they ever thought we could pull it off. However, one year later, we were in a building and had a whopping total of eight students including our three children, her son and daughter, and my daughter. We were a school of Science and World Cultures, a non-religious private school. We were a school that believed in total immersion of the students to the world and its cultures and the science behind the development of such a world. We were a school built for exploration. We developed writing skills through the reports submitted on the explorations taken. We traveled to learn. The students studied science through hands-on experiments. We had life science on campus. We incubated chickens, tadpoles, and beetles. We grew from eight students to thirty and more. We had first through eighth grades. My partner and I were enjoying every moment. The hard work never outweighed the successes. Today, I meet some of our former students on the street and at events and they still talk about how there was never a school they attended better than our school. Their parents echo them with positive affirmations regarding the quality of the education their children received. People still want to enroll their babies in the school even though it has been closed for a few years. It makes me feel good and validated.

A tragedy began somewhere around our second year of operation. My partner had cancer and it was in remission, but it reappeared. She was in the hospital for a short while during that summer, but she came out stronger than ever. She coined a phrase that I think of today, "Life is like a two-seater bicycle. God is steering in the front seat, and you are peddling in the back seat. Just keep on pedaling and have faith and God will take care of the rest." She had cancer for about four years. She was no stranger to God's mercy.

We went on for another two years growing and adding grades. We had to find a new site because we outgrew our then-current site. Once we moved into the new site, the trouble began. I was working full-time while she was working in the school as the Director. She negotiated a lease with my job for space that I knew we had to offer. She met with my boss and handled the negotiations, a big mistake to mix your job with your business. I was also selling the school to my friends and employees with children. We were growing, then another tragedy struck, cancer reappeared in another spot in her body but this time, she was under a lot of stress not just from the school.

She and I would talk about our marriages and how school was starting to take a toll on our relationships. We were both having problems. She attributed her problems to her cancer. I knew mine were a result of money and my ex-husband's inability to control my income. I was making money, more money than him, but he still wanted a say over how it was spent. I tried to increase my income, so I gave him the same amount for the bills and took out a little to help finance the school. After all, I now had two children in the school and that saved on two private school tuitions that we did not have to pay but the school needed additional support when tuition payments were slow and payables were due. My ex-husband said, "Forget that school. Let it go," but each time, he backed off a little when he saw the academic growth that was occurring in our children.

My partner got worse. She made it through that school year. That summer was not good, but she was coming back. She was getting stronger. I don't even remember if she started that school year. I just remember her going to the hospital and my bringing homemade cards from the students to her. I remember her yelling at me because as she read the names of the students, she saw a name of a student that we had agreed to get rid of. She gave me a look like you know better. I was always so humble around her that I said nothing and smiled. I went to visit her every day, waiting for the day when she would call me as always after a week or less in the hospital and would ask me to come and get her and take her home. Instead, I got a call from another Muslim sister friend who asked me to come to the hospital quickly to say my goodbye. I was in disbelief; my partner was strong. I knew she could pull through just as she had done more than once in the past but not this time. I got to the hospital minutes after she passed away. I still feel the emptiness in my soul after having lost my dearest friend. She was my hero, my confidant, my partner, and my friend.

The hardships continued and more trouble began, this time around the school space. We were in the basement of the rental facility and the main water pipe broke and destroyed almost everything we owned: computers, carpets, science equipment, library and textbooks, physical education uniforms, school sweatshirts we wore on field trips, and many others. The fire department had to come and it took more than a week to dump all the water that had stored itself in our space. They gave the school temporary housing upstairs in the same facility. Just as we began to replace our school supplies and equipment, they restored the space. They redid the floors and the walls and helped us remove all the damaged equipment and trashed it. We moved back in and resumed our regular schedule, and another rainstorm came. They called the rainstorms "El Ninyo." The rains were so strong that the pipes busted again, ruining all of what was restored and the new replacement items we had purchased. The owners of the school facility were self-insured. We asked that the school equipment and supplies be replaced as soon as possible for us to continue to educate our students. We were given temporary access to ordering supplies through the owners' purchasing system. Both the parents and staff wrote and documented all the damage to the owner's Director of Operations and Management.

The tragedies wouldn't stop, disaster struck again, this time my connection with the owners as their Finance Director was called into question, especially with the absence of my buffer, my cancer-stricken partner, it appeared as if I was the sole proprietor. Even though I had declared my relationship with the school publicly every year in writing, as a part of the legal requirement of the position I held with the company, and the fact that the school hired a point of contact person, a Director to manage the day-to-day operation, I was challenged by the owner, my boss, on the purchases that had gone through for the school as a part of the rain storm disaster damaged equipment and supply replacements. It was made to appear as if the equipment purchases were random without documentation, support, or validity. I was publicly ridiculed and openly accused of fraudulent behavior. While parents and staff could substantiate the reasons and the necessity and approval for such action, they never approached.

Things went from bad to worse. Parents were disgruntled because we had scheduled a historical excursion to the West Indies for our seventh and eighth-grade classes. The math teacher who was from Jamaica in the West Indies and the History teacher were to lead the trip. We sold dinners, candy, and pies and conducted other fundraising activities to raise money for the trip. The students and staff were excited. The math teacher had family in Jamaica where the students would stay, and he had a friend working for the airlines who promised us reduced student airfare. We had developed a budget. Parents, staff, and students worked hard to reach our fundraising goal. The Math teacher's airline fare fell through at the last second just as we had raised enough money to purchase the tickets. We raised five thousand dollars to cover the students' cost for the excursion. When we called the teacher's airline connection, they said the rates had gone up and the cost would be closer to seven thousand dollars in airfare alone. The parents and staff were devastated by the increase. We tried to reduce the number of students traveling and of course, we tried to raise more money, but the cost of the airfare was rising each day we postponed booking the flight. Jamaica, West Indies was out of our price range. Again, I stepped in. I had an uncle who lived in Saint Thomas, Virgin Islands, and I immediately called him. I asked him if we could find cheap airfare to Saint Thomas if we could stay with him, the staff, and the students. I explained what happened with the Jamaica airfare and asked him what he could do to help. He was also retired from United Airlines, and I wanted to know if he could help with a reduction in the airfare as well. United was pricier than the Jamaica airfare but my uncle tried to make arrangements for us so we could find cheap airfare to Saint Thomas. Again, I took charge. After I saw the target, I began to solve the problem; my task-driven self took over. I began asking everyone I knew, including people at work, other managers about travel agents and any airline connections they knew of. I was determined not to disappoint the students they knew of. I was determined not to disappoint the students. My friend, a manager equal to myself in authority, told me of my job as a travel agent who had helped him and other managers with their personal travel. I called the travel agent, explained the situation fully, and asked if she could find air tickets within the five-thousand-dollar range to Jamaica or Saint Thomas that fit into our travel schedule. Again, Jamaica was out of our price range, but Saint Thomas wasn't, and we booked Saint Thomas. Why was this a problem? The travel agent did business with my boss and while we had agreed to pay in full and raised the money to do so, the fraudulent perception of the activities led to additional scrutiny.

At this point, the parents were upset about the change in the excursion plans and the change in who was able to take the trip because of the escalated cost. Needless to say, it got ugly. It did not help that the parents became major participants in the demise of the school. They began to question the funds raised for the excursion to Jamaica, West Indies—how much money was raised and why they raised five thousand dollars if their child could not go and why should they pay the additional expenses when they were told the budgeted amount of money required and raised that amount for the trip. The Math teacher explained how we planned a trip around his ability to tour the students around his homeland. He explained how his friend let him down and that he could not get the students' and escorts' airfare at a reasonable rate. He further explained that we went on his advice, and we fundraised according to his estimated cost in a very conservative manner and that his lead fell through and that he understood that the students and families were disappointed. It was like his words fell on deaf ears. I explained that I had a family member living in Saint Thomas and that I explained our problem and he was working on an alternate plan. The explanations further infuriated the parents. All we had to do was find the airfare within our budget price range to take the trip. We tried online and through my contacts within my job, we found a travel agent and followed the protocol used by other employees. The school parents were unhappy because our airfare was much higher than the original estimate. We sold more lunches and pies and made up the difference. We took the graduating seniors only. Some parents wanted us to take all the middle school students. It got ugly and uglier. The facility leaseholder, my job, publicly filed legal charges against me for using their purchase orders, not their funds, for the airfare for the trip even though the airfare was paid for by the school and the insurance claims were written against the facility holder, my job, with pictures attached documenting the damage to the equipment and supplies. I was caught in a political nightmare with my job and the new political exchange of power and the parents who were yelling at me as the founder and head of the Board regarding the excursion and the exclusion of some of the middle school students. I was in the middle of a sea of controversy and trouble. The more I tried to prove to both the leasing agency, my job, and the parents the illegitimacy of their concerns, the worse it got. We took the trip and our tour guide, which my uncle set up, videoed the entire trip. The students and teacher escorts had a full-blown immersion into Saint Thomas and the surrounding islands and their culture. The math teacher who screwed up the Jamaica trip bowed out. He was humiliated and embarrassed. I went to his place to have two escorts. A parent was scheduled to go but her son was a seventh grader and she did not want to pay her airfare to go if her son was going to attend. My presence was seen as a personal vacation, not as an escort. A second lesson is the fact that perception is reality.

The trip was awesome. Our students played steel drums and they met other students and teachers playing the steel drums. They visited the schools on the Island and realized how much we had in common. They ate the native food, including fisheyes. The students spoke at their graduation of their experiences. The parents were blown away by their speeches and the video. That eighth-grade graduation represented our last graduating class. Our leasing agency, my job, went after me with a vengeance. For one year after the trip, I was publicly ridiculed, humiliated, and harassed. I was charged with criminal activities around the purchase of the tickets for the airfare and the equipment purchased after the double flooding of our school. I was seen as a criminal and a person that was stealing assets from her job to support her personal gain, her business, and the school. I learned several valuable lessons. I learned that no matter what you think and know of the truth, perception is reality. I thought the truth would guide any arguments but that was not the case. The truth was never heard. The lawyers and the newspapers took charge, and my voice was silenced. The court system took over and the battle of the lawyers began. I learned that agendas drive arguments and the truth is what people take away from the table based on what they hear. I still believe that a person's character speaks louder than the voices spoken over theirs. I applaud all those people who stood for me in the face of the allegations and never left my side. They allowed me to believe in humanity and the strength of a person's character beyond adversity and most of all, they helped restore my faith in God.

I had on rose-colored glasses. I thought that God was busy, so he gave me the brains to do what was just based on truth and doing the right thing. God wasn't busy; I was. I forgot what my deceased partner would say about the two-seater bicycle. God was in the front seat steering, and I was supposed to be in the back seat peddling. The problem was I took the front seat and started pedaling and pushed God to the back seat and gave him permission to take a break. How arrogant of me. Where was my humility? I lost all of that trying to take charge and take control of something that belonged to God. I was smacked down and publicly humiliated. Not only did I suffer but my children suffered. The newspaper stories were humiliating. Watching CNN as the discussion went on about the level of scandal occurring and the implications surrounding me, my high-level position, and the possibility of fraudulent improprieties was devastating. I was investigated for one year. I controlled approximately sixty to ninety million dollars. I was accused of misappropriating approximately eleven thousand dollars associated with the rain-damaged equipment and supplies for the school. After twelve-plus years of employment in my high-level position, this is what my tenure boiled down to. I felt belittled and betrayed. I hired an attorney, and we stayed in the legal process for about one year. While my longest stay in jail was a weekend, that was the longest weekend of my life.

I lived my life trying to stay out of jails and into God. Here I was in jail with sisters who were trapped in a lifestyle that was inconsistent with my own. I went on a hunger strike. I couldn't get out of my mind how I was arrested—three, maybe even four, police cars pulled me over in unmarked black cars. They asked me if I had weapons or drugs. I thought I ran a stop sign but I knew that couldn't be true because I wasn't in a hurry. I had just dropped my last child off at school and I was on my way home. I was un-showered, in my sweats, and I was being arrested. They searched my car like I had drugs or weapons. They put me in an unmarked car and took me to jail. They kept asking me questions about the school and the money I stole from my job. I felt like I was in the twilight zone. I kept asking for my union representative. The union supposedly had my back. While I was home being investigated for about a year, they made sure I was paid my full salary. They stayed in touch with me on a regular basis, but no one informed me of the pending arrest and the filing of criminal charges. I was in shock. I kept saying exactly what the union representative asked me to say, "I will not discuss anything without a union representative." A lot of time passed and the next thing I knew, I was taken to a jail cell. I wasn't given a phone call or anything. It was the twilight zone. After being fingerprinted and taking a mugshot, I was allowed a phone call. There was a pay phone in the cell. I called my house collection because I was worried about my children. I was renting a room to a Muslim sister who answered the phone and let me know when she came home my ex-husband, who I had been legally separated from for over a year, was sitting in my house with one of his friends. This was a shocking one because we were in the heart and heat of a heavily contested divorce and I had an active restraining order against him. He was not to be in close proximity to my house. He had the kids. To this day, I don't know how he found out what happened or how he got into my house. My suspicions tell me that my husband, who was an attorney by education and who had a lot of lawyer friends, had something to do with the city coming after me and had full knowledge of their intentions to file criminal charges. I could never prove any of the above allegations but never led me wrong.

I still remember when the divorce started. I had a nonprofit organization attorney for women's rights representing me. My ex-husband had a pit-bull female attorney who talked all kinds of shit to my attorney and went after my character. My attorney after the first session told me to get a strong attorney because she was not equipped to handle a nasty divorce like this one was turning out to. The first session was with the judge and our encounter on the court steps as we were leaving with his attorney, who basically told me if I didn't quit and turn over my assets, she would go after me personally, my job, and the school. I politely told her to kiss my ass, but I never forgot the threat. The divorce kept getting uglier and uglier. His attorney was ruthless in the courtroom. I kept asking friends for a good divorce attorney and I kept looking until I found a pit-bull attorney to match his. My divorce attorney was relentless. Just as he was going in for the kill, I was arrested.

My life was spiraling downhill. I had a divorce attorney and now a criminal attorney. I was arrested on a Friday and all my money was in my bank accounts under my name. The police had seized my purse with my ATM card, and I could not give anyone power of attorney because I did not have an attorney and my friends did not have access to legal documents on a weekend. I was up the creek without any paddles. I called my family in New York, and I gave them my friend's numbers locally to call. They worked hard all weekend. My bail was ten thousand dollars. None of my friends knew what that meant. They were trying to find ten thousand dollars to post the bail, but everyone was having a problem because, during this time, the banks were closed on the weekend. They did a personal collection, and they got the bail money, but the bail bonds person told them not to waste their money to leave me there until Monday and hire an attorney instead. Until they approached the bail bonds person, none of us realized that the bond amount was actually one thousand dollars. I called my family in New York. They were the only ones that would accept calls from jail. My family was already in communication with my best friends locally and they mutually agreed that I should stay in the city jail until Monday. I was pissed. I could have killed everyone for assuming the hell hole I was in was okay for me for a weekend. I dare not cry and let the other inmates know my weakness. I sucked it up and went on a hunger strike. I ate nothing and I prayed my Muslim prayers. Monday finally arrived and I met the judge for the first time. I had an attorney standing there representing me and the judge gave the order to release me. I thought I was going to leave that minute but that is not how it works. I went back to my cell. I was waiting for them to call my name when they came. It wasn't to release me but to take me to the county jail. You see, I spent the weekend in the city jail. I went on the bus with the other inmates to the county jail, while the women's bus was not full. I watched them herd brother after brother into a couple of buses. I remember thinking this is where our brothers are. They were like cattle, short ones, tall ones, handsome, and young on their way to do some time. I was blown away by the trip to the county jail. I was on the same freeway I drove everyday to work, and I passed my home. When I passed my home, I saw that familiar yellow house with white trimming. I broke down and cried. I knew this was bad and I knew my babies were never going to be the same. I knew I was leaving my safe world for something I had no idea about other than the stories I was told on the steps of my neighbor's house by her hoodlum jailbird cousin. I was entering a world that I never wanted to be a part of.

Once we arrived, they stripped us of our clothes. We put on orange suits. Then they sent us to a large cell. The women were across the hallway from the men, but we could see each other from the nurse's office. We all had to see the nurse. They stripped me of my shirt while the men watched and did catcalls. Then, they took me to my cell. I shared my cell with three or five other women. It is hard for me to remember how many, but I know it was a small number. The jail was state-of-the-art. It looked brand new. I remember telling the jailers that I was not supposed to be there and that I was going to be released any moment. They had the typical comment which was, "Yeah, just like everyone else here. You all are going to be released at some time." I still remember one of my cellmates just vomiting all over herself. She was like a fountain of vomit. She was hooked on heroin, and she was going through withdrawals. She was not older than twenty. The other inmates and I tried to help her, but she was beyond our help. Eventually, she just laid on the floor in her own vomit. Then the guard came in. She was talking shit while she gave me the same words as everyone else. Finally, a separate guard came to the cell and called my name. She said, "You are going to be released." The guard with the plastic gloves chuckled and said, "You just missed out on the fun." I am starting my strip search. I thanked God and went with the jailer. She gave me my funky clothes that I had spent the weekend in to change into. I never felt so good about the sight of my things. I didn't care what they smelled like. They were mine. I went to a release area, and I looked outside. It was dark. I had no sense of time. My housemate was standing there with open arms, and I cried like I was a baby who had lost their parents for days on end and had just found them.

Shortly, after I arrived home, one of my favorite uncles from Saint Thomas came to take care of me and help me through all of this. He lived with me for over a year. That is how long it took to get through the criminal activities and the divorce. The job stopped paying once they filed criminal charges. My house note went unpaid and while I had equity in the property, I could not refinance. My ex-husband's attorney slapped a lien on my property to stop me from selling or refinancing. This was a nasty divorce. I had to figure out a way to save the house. I could only save it through bankruptcy. I was hiring my third attorney, a bankruptcy attorney. I was trying to find a job but the pending criminal charges and the very public newspaper blurbs on me were not helping me with employment. I filed for unemployment, and I started doing additional odd and end jobs to supplement my income. I was never shy of working. I would do whatever legal job I could find to take care of my family. I was a courier for several months. I drove and picked up all kinds of equipment and bank packages at different times of the night. Sometimes, I would have to put my children in the car with me if my uncle had to fly home to take care of some business matters. I was determined to survive.

MY ATTORNEYS

I met with the bankruptcy attorney, who was referred to me by my divorce attorney. We discovered that for six years, no taxes were filed while I was married. In order for my bankruptcy to be filed, I would have to file those taxes. I checked with my divorce attorney, and I ended up filing those taxes married filing separately. Oh! I just could not get a break.

I filed the bankruptcy which was dismissed but I saved the house for a moment. Foreclosure was imminent. Then God sent me an angel. I told him my story and he offered to give me a loan to buy my ex-husband's portion of his community property in the house. We set up a meeting. My uncle, I, my ex-husband, and a friend attended the meeting. I explained that this was my house, but I understood community property laws and I wanted to strike a deal. I was willing to pay him half of the accrued equity in the house in cash. He refused. A second meeting was set up with my angel and my ex-husband at the escrow office to try to settle a buy-out and have my ex-husband release the lien. We waited and waited until he never showed up. The house was foreclosed on, but my angel brought it off the city hall steps while my ex-husband stood at the sale and watched. I could not bear to go. I turned it over to God and went on with my life. I received a phone call from my angel on the day of the foreclosure sale after the time of the sale had passed. He told me that he owned my house. He made a promise to me that if I got my life back together, he would give me the house back at cost. Again, I cried like a baby, and this time, I remembered to thank God. You see, all this turmoil made me turn to the person I should have turned to from the beginning. My uncle always said to me,

"Let go and let God." I began to pray every time I got weary. I found out that God answers prayers.

The criminal charges were still pending. I went back and forth to court for about a year and a half with my uncle by my side. I had a lot of well-wishers and active supporters who believed in me. I am so thankful for all of them because when I felt like all was lost, they kept on fighting. They became vocal and visible, and they were my angels. Finally, we reached an impasse, and it was all over. The school was closed and all that was left of it were my memories. To this day, I don't know what happened to all of the equipment that was in the leased spaces. I suppose the equipment alone totaled about $20,000 more than the criminal charges. It was disposed of and never a letter or an accounting of it was given to any member of the school. It is amazing how one-sided the world can be when you are the one being attacked. I let go of this. My uncle wanted me to file a civil suit, but I was tired and beaten down. I had enough. God had answered my prayers and I did not want to put my family through any more ridicule and exposure. Sometimes, I wish I was stronger and stood up and fought a little harder, but the lessons I have learned far outweigh the money I could have made from the civil suit. I believe in the saying, "You have to pick and choose your battles. Every battle is not worth fighting." I still had to get through the divorce that I put on hold. I said goodbye to my criminal attorney, and I reopened my divorce case with my divorce attorney.

SAVING MY CHILD

My now high school teenage daughter went absolutely crazy. Again, I thought I was holding it all together. I thought that my children were faring well. I pulled them closer to me. I put my youngest daughter, who was going to my school when it abruptly shut down in a family-based school and had social consciousness as a guide for education, a very similar philosophy to my school. My youngest son was in a Muslim school. My teenage daughter was in a tragedy. She had gone to my school and graduated from our middle school. My school at that time was grades one through eight. The teenage daughter had spent all of her life in private schools but the divorce forced me to take her out of her private high school and place her in a public high school for the first time in her life. I thought I was beating the odds by using someone else's address to put her in a good school district. I was successful in getting her in. I used a Muslim sister's address in the city I wanted her to attend public high school. I would not dare put her in the schools in my city. They had a bad reputation for violence and poor-quality education. While there were some success stories, the statistics on the test scores and the percentage of students going on to college were unreal and pitiful. I wasn't going to subject my child to any of it. So, off she went to a school larger than she had ever been in. This was her sophomore year. She was a B-/C+ student who had plenty of room for improvement. Her guidance counselor and I decided that she should be placed in at least two honors classes to make up the difference from the private school academic level of her former school and to match their equivalent primary classes. I was driving her to school every day. Then the criminal charges filed against me hit the newspaper. I started not just driving her to school but picking her up from school as well, trying to shelter her from the disgrace and pain. I thought I was on top of everything. I was juggling the balls and keeping them all up in the air even though my world was crashing all around me. I would drive three children to different schools, go to work, and pick all three children up from school. I was always late picking up my teenage daughter, but I felt she was the oldest, so she could wait while I picked up the two younger children. Boy, was I wrong? She was meeting and greeting all the street people. She soon convinced me that she could sometimes take the bus home because I was running so late. I said okay. I thought she was maturing. You know I thought she was becoming responsible and was trying to help her struggling single parent out, take some of the load off. We were three months into the school year, and I had not seen a report card. I couldn't ask the school because they were mailing the report cards home, but home was the Muslim sister's house. Every time I drove by her house, she wasn't home. It got to a point where I began asking my teenage daughter to talk with her daughter who was attending the school and ask her to bring the report card to school with her. In retrospect, I couldn't understand why my daughter could never find her daughter to make the exchange. Soon, teachers began to call me at home asking for a parent conference. I would go to the school to talk to her honors teachers who were mostly concerned with my daughter's missing assignments. I would go off on my daughter and stay in touch with the teachers to see if she was getting on top of her work. We had weekly phone conference calls and sometimes, I would make a surprise visit to the school to talk with her teachers. The teachers never bothered to tell me that the reason she was so behind was that she hardly ever came to class. When I finally went to the school and asked for a copy of her first semester grades, she had flunked every class with the exception of one and that grade was a "D." She had about forty-five absences from school even though I was driving her and picking her up from school every day. I pulled her out of the school and tried teaching her myself through independent study homeschool classes. My uncle lived with me, so I had a built-in Gestapo, a second pair of eyes and ears. She was home and beginning to produce some academic work. I had trouble finding proctors/teachers for her independent study classes.

I was trying to teach the classes myself and work and take care of my two younger children. It was another formula for disaster. My daughter needed to do research on some of her assignments. I thought she had at least one serious-minded academically strong friend that she could go with to the library and do exactly as instructed. But as I sat at work thinking she was in the public library three blocks away, she and her friend were in the drug store six blocks away from my job stealing candy and milk with money in their pockets and getting caught by a security guard. I was in shock when the phone rang and it was the security officer from the drug store informing me that he had my child and her friend in custody. I left my job and arrived at the store immediately after the call. I could tell from the look on their faces that they were guilty as charged. I knew then that a freight train was about to run over my child. A freight train called the urban streets, and my daughter was just going to be a statistic, just like all the other black children who choose the streets instead of hard work and academics. I cried many nights and one morning, I woke up and knew that I had to do something drastic. I had to get my baby, my teenage daughter, out of the urban streets. I began calling and asking questions of friends with children with similar lifestyles and with girls my daughter's age. I wanted to know if I was alone, if they were experiencing the same pain, and to my surprise they were. They all had different solutions but the one that rang a bell for me was a boarding school. While boarding school was never an option for any black families, I knew growing up in an urban city, it was the one thing I remember my mother faintly taunted me with when I was out of control, but I knew it was just a threat because I didn't know one black person that ever went to boarding school as a kid. When I was a kid, there were boys that got shipped off to military school, but everybody knew military school was for boys.

I had one Muslim sister begin to tell me about her daughter and her troubles in our neighborhood urban high school and what she did about it. She put her in a boarding school not in California but on the East Coast, Connecticut. I cried as I told her the story about my teenage daughter, what I had experienced with her and the things I had tried to turn it around. She understood and she gave me the phone number for the admissions director of her daughter's boarding school. I called the Director and we talked for a long time. He scheduled an appointment. I scheduled a flight and packed my daughter's bags, and we flew to the East Coast. I picked up my mother in New York and the three of us drove to Connecticut for my daughter's interview. I didn't care about the money. I wanted to save my daughter. I refused to let her become a victim of the urban streets. I called my estranged husband and let him know of my plans. I gave him the website of the school and I asked if he had any questions. He knew like I did that there was something wrong with our daughter and that it was just a matter of time before she would be gone beyond the point of return. We set aside our hatred and put our child first.

That school was HYDE. Instead of the school just saving my daughter, it saved me as well. Both my daughter and I graduated from her boarding school with honors. My daughter went on to a four-year college and I went on to discover my passion in life for working with nonprofit organizations in my own business and for writing. I am thankful to God for taking the time to save two wretches like her and me. My journey through boarding school was therapeutic and spiritual. Today, I have forgiveness in my heart and faith beyond faith. I truly know and understand that God is in control of everything and that I don't need to be superwoman and juggle all the balls in the air. I just practiced letting go and letting God. He has brought my daughter and I through hell and back. I later learned that my daughter was hanging around with a drug dealer who was her boyfriend. He had her selling drugs on the street and more. I didn't have a clue about any of this. I just knew my heart was troubled and that was how I was moved to make a drastic change to save my child.

MY DIVORCE AND AFTER

My uncle and I set up a meeting with my divorce attorney. I had kept him abreast of the criminal proceedings and he too was an angel. He held my case in abeyance until the criminal proceedings were over. We set up a new court date with the judge. Prior to going to court, we discovered that my ex-husband's attorney petitioned to remove herself from the case. My ex-husband was representing himself. My attorney was sharp; he left his fangs behind but not his wit and experience. I played legal assistant to his law clerk to keep the cost down and we went forward. I was pleased with the outcome. Most of all, I was pleased to be divorced. I felt as if God was slowly giving me my life back. I made a promise to God at that point to remember to go after my passion, never forget the lessons learned, and to have faith, most of all to have faith because God answers prayers.

I went from a complete disaster in my life to trying to rebuild after an earthquake. My metaphor was my home was demolished. I had no insurance, no job, but I had the land and God. I had the foundation for something great. I have been in the business of rebuilding ever since. A second angel was always there but I never noticed him. I was his boss and he in all the turmoil was becoming my friend. He grew on me. He had a weird sense of humor. He would call and tell me every time my name was on the paper. He would take annoying segments of the articles written and remind me of little things like how old I was as written in the paper. He would have been considered ruthless and non-sympathetic but instead, he was like one of those crazy mixed-up satires. I knew he was mocking the paper more than me and his jokes prepared me for my neighbors and my acquaintances that were reading the same stories. He created lightheartedness inside of me which shielded me from taking myself and this media attack too seriously. I grew to appreciate his lopsided humor. I grew to appreciate his friendship. Then I was faced with a new trauma. My house angel wanted and needed out. He needed me to find someone to take over the loan on my house. It was too soon for me to take it back because even though my divorce was final, and how the judge told my ex-husband if someone decides to sell her the house tomorrow, it will be her house if she can buy it. My credit was shot. I could not buy the house back yet. I needed another angel. I prayed and God sent me someone. He took the house from the first angel at cost and held the house at cost until I was ready to qualify to take it over. I had solicited a great credit repair company referred to me by a bank that I was trying to finance the house with. I hired them and for two years, they worked on repairing my credit. Finally, I met a woman loan officer at my son's basketball team practice. I began to explain what I wanted to do, which was to buy my house back, and the fact that I was working on credit repair for the past two years. She was a divorced woman who had lost her home and equal assets in her divorce. She wanted to give back to another woman who experienced the same tragedies as she experienced, a case of women helping women. She was another angel. I didn't think I was ready, but she proved me wrong. Today, I am the owner of my house. Again, I am thankful to God for giving me faith. I was finally applying what my uncle always said, "Let go and let God." Through all my experiences, I learned that God will only move mountains if you get out of the way and leave it up to him.

MOVING ONTO THE
HEALING PROCESS

No more attorneys, no more ball juggling, but a lot of faith and understanding of God's role in my life.

WITH SUCCESS COMES RESPONSIBILITY. YOU HAVE TO STEP UP. YOU HAVE TO PERFORM. YOU CAN'T RUN. YOU CAN'T HIDE

ATTITUDE—a piece written by Charles Swindoll, *"The longer I live, the more I realize the impact of attitude on life. Attitude, to me, is more important than facts; it is more important than the past, than education, than money, than circumstances, than failures, than successes, than what other people think or say or do. It is more important than appearance, giftedness, or skill. It will make or break a company... a church... a home. The remarkable thing is we have a choice every day regarding the attitude we will embrace for that day. We cannot change our past... We cannot change the fact that people will act in a certain way. We cannot change the inevitable. The only thing we can do is play on the one string we have and that is our attitude... I am convinced that life is 10% what happens to me and 90% how I react to it, and, so it is with you... We are in charge of our ATTITUDES."*

My work done at my daughter's boarding school was a piece titled Personal Journey:

What am I learning about myself? My issues are controlling the outcome and learning to release control. I spend time trying to label my children as something other than what they are. I am working on honesty as a family principle that I will hold in high regard. First, I had to learn that letting go of the reins and beginning to trust the process is a part of the rebuilding process. I had to focus on taking more risks without trying to think through all the possible outcomes. The strengthening of my faith still remains an obstacle. I continue to work on my relationship with all my children. I must stop trying to take care of others as much and begin to focus on myself.

Is there an area in my life that I do not want to take hold of?

There are several: one of which is taking risks, learning to stay in fun and joy of the risk, and not going back to what I know works and the security of what works. Also, once I am at risk, I become clumsy and I can't define my security. I have to ask for help. I'm not sure it's going to work. I feel as if people are waiting to define my risk- taking as stupid and foolish. My age becomes a factor and a deterrent. What helps is staying in faith trusting that a higher power will bless me and reward me for my actions. I began to trust that my actions would result in success. The other fear I have is taking hold of my health. I love to exercise daily but I overeat often and spend a lot of my time being angry with myself about my weight gain. Most times, I am disgusted with my physical appearance. My fear of being noticed and seen as physically attractive continue to override my attempts to control my weight issues. I believe my unwillingness to be seen as physically attractive has a lot to do with the sexual abuse I experienced at a young age. I don't think I have ever forgiven myself for feeling any good feelings about the abuse. I think somewhere in my mind deep in the crevices of my consciousness is a fear that I wanted to be abused and that my physical appearance made the abuse occur. How do I move beyond my childhood self to an adult who understands and forgives? Do I let my fears override my desire to be thin and healthy? As a result of my childhood, I remain a giver and not a taker. I am at fault. There must be balance. I want to make the world a better place and I receive joy from seeing relief from other people's pain. I like making others happy. I am learning to take by asking others for help and by receiving their help without feeling the need to give in return. I am learning to take and receive help from others.

More Hyde school work—Title: The Truth of My Life (December 09, 2004)— telling the story as an adult.

What are the important moments in my life? What are the issues? Who are the important people? Despite it all, I was happy as a child. I lived in a small community of families that knew one another well. I went to school with my next-door neighbors until I was in high school. Besides being bullied in middle school, being sexually abused by my brother, and remaining a tomboy until high school, I tried to remain happy.

High school was my worst school experience. I hated being bused to school. I spent 45 minutes to one-and-a-half hours one way to school. The white people hated me for invading their community. I remembered their anger outside of the school doors and the surrounding community. I remembered the fifth-class treatment by my teachers and the administrators inside the doors of the school. It was OK after the first year because it was at that point in my life that I decided I could prove the world wrong and make a difference. I was determined to make them eat crow.

In college, my determination grew stronger. It was an all-white environment with few minorities. But the turning point was in high school with the death of my father. My father was a brilliant man, way ahead of his time. He lied his way into the service at sixteen or seventeen years old after he graduated from high school. He was a career soldier who I never really knew until I entered middle school. That was when he left the armed services and came home to live with us. He was a weekend alcoholic, and I was his guardian angel. I had a love-hate relationship with him.

He died and I finally could stop taking care of him and protecting my family from him. I remember waking in the middle of the night to make sure he had not set the house on fire. In addition to his serious drinking problem, he loved to smoke cigarettes. I can still smell them today, Camel cigarettes, and see that cream-colored package with the brown Camel on the front. He would fall asleep with the cigarette in his hand and burn holes in the couch. I would wake up in the night, take the cigarettes from his hand, and hide their remaining package of cigarettes in the cabinet way off so he couldn't find them. I was determined to keep us and him alive.

My two older brothers were failures in my father's eyes. I was determined to be the success story. Upon my father's death, determination and focus kicked in.

I no longer had the pressure of taking care of my father. My mother became very dependent on me. My brothers were not business-minded people. They were too wrapped up in themselves and their own lives to spend time with my mom. She needed help with managing our father's death and her finances after his death. My oldest brother was concerned with his new marriage. My youngest brother was consumed with his friends and the streets. That left me—I was the answer. I could think independently. I was business-minded. It was insightful and a very old spirit. My mom wanted me to take over the business of running the family. I was eighteen and very tired. I had already spent too many years being forced to grow up and take care of my father. I did not want to do it again. I wanted out. I didn't want to abandon it, but I wanted to distance myself. I set forth a plan to graduate from a local two-year college and then attend a four-year college and graduate. I wanted to attend a four-year college that was far away in Minnesota. I decided to stay a safe distance away, on Long Island. I was an hour and a half away from my mother. Finally, I was far enough to live my life without having to take care of others. I was close enough to come home and check to see how things were going but far enough to be independent.

Some years passed and I reached success by graduating from college. I began to change my goals; I yearned for family life. My first goal was a husband and a family, and I got a husband and a family. My second goal was to have my own business. I got my own business. Then my goals shifted to just having good-paying jobs. I got good-paying jobs. *Success for me equaled determination.* I wanted to own a school and educate my children. I owned the school, and I educated my children.

Then all the failures came at once, divorce, and I lost the school and my good-paying job. Determination equaled failure. *I discovered that even with my determination, I could not control the world.*

The harmony of my life—What are the important moments in my life? What are the issues? Who are the important people?

While I was strong and independent inside my home, I was shy and introverted outside of my home. I had eczema, a very bad skin disease, until I was sixteen. I was teased a lot. My nickname was Itchy Ball. Certain areas of my body appeared to be burnt as a result of my skin disease. Just as my skin would begin to clear up, I would break out again with a change in season. When I started my menstrual cycle, my mother found a wonderful German doctor who understood eczema and my skin cleared. I became what boys considered hot. I went from the ugly teased duckling in junior high school to someone boys wanted to date. I became very scared, and I began to eat and gain weight. *I noticed that the more weight I gained, the less attention I received. I was safe again in my shy-introverted life.*

In junior high school, because I was shy, I was picked on and bullied a lot. Being bullied taught me something. *I learned to find friends and get along even when I did not like my life.*

I learned early on that fighting and arguing could never bring about good results. I argued with my dad a few days before his death. And that argument was the first and only argument we ever had. The day I came home sick from menstrual cramps and angry with my dad from the argument we had earlier in the week, I ignored him.

He was sick and not feeling well today. I barely stopped to look at him because I was so angry. Instead, I went straight to my room. After falling asleep, my mother arrived home shortly thereafter. I was awakened by her screams. I still hear her screams as if it was yesterday. She screamed, "Lomenka, come here. I think your father is dead." When I finally awoke from her screams, I rushed downstairs to discover her words were true. My father was lying in his bed cold, stiff, and very peaceful. He had been dead for hours. It was as if he knew he was going to die. He opened the window. He lay across the bed and went to sleep. He died and I could finally stop taking care of him. But it was unfair because I wanted his death. I wanted my freedom. All of a sudden, I received what I wished for and had secretly been asking for. You see, I wanted to be free of taking care of him. The sadness that came from his death was the realization that I had lost not only my father but my best friend. He died without calling me for help and without saying goodbye. We argued because I refused to accept his nasty behavior and his abusive language in our house. I was tired of his alcoholic behavior, and I was finally strong enough to speak out. A few days later, he died. ***So, what I learned is that being submissive and subservient keeps the people you love around.***

In my marriage, I chose to be submissive and subservient to my husband. I chose my children's happiness and my family's togetherness over my own happiness.

What I didn't understand about my children then is embodied in a simple statement, "Your children come through you, but they are not from you." I didn't understand that my children, my husband, and myself all have souls, a conscience, and the ability to make choices.

"Love hurts too much."

LETTER FROM MY SIXTEEN-YEAR-OLD DAUGHTER

Dear Mom,

This weekend has been a good weekend for me. I have gone inside myself to find the courage I needed to finally ask you about your past. I am so glad you finally opened up and told me. But I question why it took so long and was it a trust issue? As a child, I remember myself having such a good relationship with you. I am starting to believe it is because I was blinded by things. When I got older and my eyes began to see the past, the surface of things, is when I began to notice we started to grow apart. It was like a cycle. I remember being young and watching you slowly push my older brother out of your life and then my older sister. I remember feeling like it was not going to happen to me but slowly, it did. I will never forget the day I was really hurt when you were disciplining me and I told you I felt like I could not talk to you and you said, "Our closeness and friendship are not the most important thing." I know you said it because you were more concerned about my safety than our relationship. I always felt that it is easier for you to push someone away rather than love.

I know that one of my biggest struggles in life is to struggle openly. Which I think ties into the reason why for a while it was so easy for me to be dishonest with myself and others. Because I never wanted anyone to know how I felt. You are a very independent woman and I love and respect that about you. But it angers me that you're being this way has affected so much of my life. You never allow yourself to be vulnerable and I think taking risks is a big part of life. I also feel that with your independence comes intimidation. I think that is a part of the reason it has taken me so long to tell you these things because I fear your reaction and not meeting your expectations for me. It hurts to come to the realization that until now, most of my accomplishments have been from other people or because someone had to force me to do it. I have never done things for myself. I know that I have been too much of a crutch for my younger sister. I think I get it from you being too much of a crutch for me when I was young…

Love U Mom

A Letter to My Grandmother,

Dear Grandma,

It never occurred to me to write you this letter until I began writing this book. I just wanted you to know how much I love you. My life would not be what it is today without your gentle guidance. From a baby looking for someone to reach out and talk to and to just be there when no one else would listen, you were there. Always patiently listening and always knowing the right thing to say. As I write this letter, tears fill up my eyes because I never had the chance to say thank you and show you just how much I loved you. You were and are still my hero. You knew more than you could ever tell but you still took care of making sure I felt safe and loved.

I remember my phone calls to you after I received what I called then an unfair and unjust whipping. I remember asking permission to call you and my mother saying, "Yes, go ahead." It was almost like you were waiting by the phone for my call. You would answer and I would just start crying and you would wait patiently for me to calm down and I would start talking, the words would flow like a river going downstream. You would just listen and when I was done, you would say some words that would automatically calm me down and I would hang up and everything felt like it was okay once again. I loved you because you understood the child in me that was crying silently to be heard and loved.

I loved my summers with you in that crowded big house with us sleeping on top of each other, but the best part was being with you and my favorite girl cousins. I just had my brothers, and my mother was as girly as the boy next door. I had my girlfriends but they had sisters and cousins and their own family drama. It was just hard trying to hang out beyond jumping rope, hanging out braiding hair, learning the newest dances, and chatting about who you liked and didn't like in the neighborhood or school. Sure, we got in trouble together, but we couldn't really spend the night over at each other's houses because we lost our privilege to hang out tomorrow. I looked forward to having a place to stay that wasn't my cramped room with my 2 brothers. I think you knew I needed the break and I loved that you created the space for all of us to have a special summer home.

Then there were our special conversations when you came in from work where we lived together in your bed and just talked. Wow, I loved those moments and I loved the fact that I think they were as important to you as they were to me. I never knew I was special to you until after your death when my uncles told me how much you talked about me and how much you loved me and how special I was to you. I just knew that no matter where I was and no matter what was going on in my life, you were just a phone call away.

When I sit back and reflect on our relationship, I know my uncles were right. When you took time off your jobs to travel every summer, I was there beside you as if I was a piece of your luggage. We traveled down south and to Washington, DC to see your sister. We made the trips almost every summer until I became a teenager and I wanted my own space. My oldest brother moved and now it was just my youngest brother and I left. I still didn't stay home much. I would visit my cousin. She was a year younger than me, but we were best friends. Her mother, my older cousin, was a single parent with a big house. I would spend most of my weekends over at their house but I never stopped calling and checking in and talking about my feelings as I was growing up and becoming a woman and you were growing with me. Our conversations were intensifying but always with love and your gentleness. I remember when I called to tell you I was going to Paris and London and I knew no one but I had a few friends that were going to travel with me. Then, those friends backed out and I revealed that I was traveling to England with someone but I was going to Paris alone. I remember your reaction was, "I can't talk you out of it, but I will ask you to keep in touch with me and/or your mom once you arrive." As usual, your reaction was perfect and apropos for. You're the same person you watched me grow into. You knew me so well. Thank you, Grandma, thank you for being you and allowing me to be me. I know you are one of my guardian angels. I just want to make you and God proud.

Love,
Your granddaughter.

LESSONS LEARNED THROUGH & FROM EXPERIENCE

I learned not to love unconditionally, why, because my dad left without even saying goodbye. I chose harmony over truth because my dad was so angry with me. He never asked me for help while dying. He just died. I've discovered that your true feelings don't matter if they hurt others. I decided to never let people hear the truth because they can't handle the truth and they will make choices to shut you out and leave you. Instead, I chose to be self-reliant. My mother became very needy. She wanted me to take charge. I was the child that took care of the family. She pleaded with me to stay home so I went to college close by. I didn't like my mother at that time. I felt she had ignored me all of my life up until the time after my father's death, but I responded to her request.

I decided I had never wanted to be like my mother. She was unable to take care of our family business without the help of other people. I never understood this, and my own independence would not allow me to tolerate such behavior.

My independence was part of my nature but was a learned behavior from a mentor, my grandmother. Next to my father, my grandmother was the other person in my life who I loved and was my friend.

The other thing I learned from my father's death is that love could not fix everything. I learned that all the sympathy from all the people who loved him could not bring him back. I also learned that all my requests to God could not and did not bring my father back. *I lost my faith in God when I lost my father.*

"The key people in my life since childhood that had an impact on my life."

My high school-age daughter since she has been at Hyde, the boarding High School, has helped to reshape my view of love. She has forced me to look at my inability to have emotion and affection. She has shown me that what I called love was not enough. She challenged me to change. She made me see that it is okay to hug someone and say I love you. At first, the change was awkward. Saying I love you to my children felt stupid and unnecessary. Hugging them felt awkward. Little by little, *I am growing to say the words I love effortlessly and to give hugs sporadically because it just feels good.*

My ex-husband challenges me with my ability to trust. I shared my darkest secrets with him. I tried to learn to love him unconditionally. I tried to develop my spiritual connection with God through him and with him. *Each time in each experience, he taught me that I was not good enough.*

With my secrets, he taught me that people will use your darkness to hold you hostage. He kept me believing that because the things in my past happened to me, I would never be capable of loving anyone. He led me to believe that I was a terrible lover and that I would never be better. My self-esteem was so low that I valued the opinions of the people closest to me more than my own.

I tried to love him because he was my husband and the father of my children. He made me see my inadequacies as a wife and mother. After years of verbal abuse from him, I began to believe that I wasn't good enough and would never be good enough. I began to resent him. I began to question my love for him. *I learned that unconditional love was stupid and painful.* His actions further reinforced that unconditional love is not worth giving because it will be abused and mistreated.

I accepted Islam with my husband. He spent years trying to convince me that he was the person I should seek knowledge from when trying to understand the religion. I came to Islam, and I met a wonderful mentor who was teaching a class at our local masjid. This brother, my mentor, was whistle full of love and joy and it exploded from all parts of his body as he spoke and taught Islam. There was no question I had that he could not answer to my satisfaction. He made me feel at ease with religion and with myself. I decided to accept Islam as a result of my mentor and my reading of the Quran. Even though I explained my feelings to my husband, he insisted that he should be the source of my knowledge when it came to understanding Islam. His feeling about my mentor brought about tension in our marriage because we were both Muslim and dedicated to our religion. Even with his strong sentiments, I continued to seek out others for their wisdom and knowledge of Islam. I became a stronger and more devout Muslim as a result of my studies. My husband felt offended not only because I went to others for knowledge but because I began to challenge him on his understanding and interpretation of the religion. When I wouldn't conform to the way he felt a Muslim and a woman should be, then I was not a Muslim in his eyes. I began to crumble under his pressure. I began to question my faith in Allah and my understanding of the Quran. I stopped studying religion. I stopped going to the masjid. I gave up teaching Islam to my children. *All in all, once again, I gave up my relationship with God.*

After the divorce ... My future looks very bright without my ex-husband in it. I am rediscovering myself and my relationship with God. As I explore a new relationship with my boyfriend, I am trying to forgive all the people and the pain from my past. *I am learning to push and to be pushed. I am learning to explore my sexuality and I'm allowing myself to be explored. I am learning that opinions are just opinions, and I can take them or leave them. It is my choice.*

"MY WORLD THEN AND MY WORLD NOW."

A quick synopsis of my world, my dad's funeral, my mother, my brothers and me, our feelings at that time: love hurts too much, love just hurts, and I learned to choose harmony over truth. I could have saved my dad if I didn't say a hurtful truth to him. I chose self-reliance. I knew not to be needy like my mother. I also learned that love of and from others could not fix things.

I went on to college to discover that success is easy. Once I learned the key that opens the door to good grades and achievement in college, I was on my way.

I finally moved far away from my family. I moved to San Francisco. I secured my independence. No one could reach me now to ask me to take care of them. I began to learn more keys to success. I learned more self-reliance. Family could only visit from a distance. I felt free.

Success again, I married and had a family. I found a religion. This success begins to dwindle. As the marriage began to fail, I felt reinforced by my original thoughts that love was not safe. I began to feel small, unattractive, and unworthy. Again, I lost my faith in God.

My world began to crash even more. My keys to success disappeared. My family life was crushed by the divorce. My family ideals were gone. My children lost and I was lost. I lost my husband. I lost my job. I lost my business. I lost my dreams. My world as I knew it crashed.

My family came to the rescue. My uncle came from New York to live with me and help me through my problems. I prayed and cried. I still had a sense of relief because I did not have to go it alone. This was a time in my life that I can truly say I appreciated my family. Because my uncles believe in God, he helped me to resurrect my spiritual self. He was a gift from God. My spiritual self was being reborn.

"My work on me."

"My letter to me."

Letter written to me by me:

> Lomenka,
>
> You're such a loving and caring individual. You have a lot of dreams and aspirations. You seem the least sure when it comes to love. Your compassion is there for others but not for you. You must learn to trust others to give you their love. You must learn to receive their love with the same compassion that you give to others.
>
> You are so insightful into the lives of others. Learn to receive their criticism of you. Trust their wisdom. Know and value yourself as a worthy, deserving woman. Follow your dreams. Make your visions a part of your world but do this with love and compassion for yourself and others.
>
> Your past has held you hostage to loving. Cry your tears. Forgive yourself and know that we all make mistakes. Also, know that it's okay to love someone so much that you show anger at them for not taking care of themselves. It was okay for you to tell your father your feelings even if you had to say it in anger. You gave your father the gift of letting him know that you cared, and his behavior was unacceptable. When you love

someone, you can display anger, hurt, and pain. You can yell and scream. You must learn to forgive yourself for not having the opportunity to say you're sorry. God took your father when it was his time to leave this earth. It is unfortunate that his death occurred before you both had an opportunity to apologize to each other. God is in control, not you. You have to let go of your sadness. You have to thank God for providing your dad with a beautiful resting place as a solution to his despair. You need to be thankful for your father's blessings and move on.

You need to embrace your dreams and stop letting the past hold you back. Take the risk and don't worry about the outcome. You are special and deserving of all your dreams. You can achieve love and allow others to give their love to you. Don't be afraid of emotion and affection. Instead, embrace them and make them a part of you. Love for the sake of loving and trust in the process.

Letter to my deceased father…

Dear Dad,

One time, your friend called me when he brought you home. I remember being about twelve or thirteen years old. I made a real loud sigh so that all my friends could hear my unhappiness with having to stop playing to take care of you. I remember your friend chastising me and saying, "That's your father and don't ever do that to him," and from that day forward, I watched for the car to see if I needed to help you without one gesture of unhappiness or anger. I just did my job and made sure you were okay.

I was so glad when Mom finally convinced you to stop driving. I was tired of riding with you in the car from grandma's house on the other side of town, home. You were drunk and I was praying for our safety and making sure you stayed awake long enough to get us home safely. Dad, you turned a fifteen-minute drive from Grandma's house into a five-minute drive. You showed your skill by driving on two wheels around that famous light pole by the hospital. It was okay because I knew when I saw that light pole, we would be home in a matter of seconds. You know as soon as we arrived home, Mom would call grandma to let her know we arrived safely. It got to the point that I was the only one courageous enough to ride with you. Dad, I really loved you and I wanted to make sure you were safe.

Dad, don't ever get so sick that you DTs, your alcohol withdrawals return again. You scared me when you barricaded the doorway and pulled your gun on the imaginary soldiers standing outside our house. Dad, you wouldn't let Mom talk to you and I tried to talk to you while I was crying and sobbing. I wanted you to listen to me. I finally got you to put the gun down while Mom was calling the police. Dad, when the men in the white coats took you away, I didn't want them to harm you. I didn't want you to leave me.

I love you, Dad, and I always will love you.

Love You Always,
Your Daughter & Friend,
Lomenka

Sharing my struggles and breaking the cycle . . .

My inability to let go of my silent anger with my mom has been one of my struggles. I wrote a letter during a family-sharing weekend at my seventeen-year-old daughter's school. I read the letter to my mom at her home in New York, the house I grew up in. I told her everything that was holding me back and the ways in which I was like her.

Taking a risk and making a change...

A risk for me is telling my children about my boyfriend, who he is, and shifting my relationship to a more public open relationship with my family.

What behavior will I model for me and my family ...

I am trying my best to model the truth in my family relationships. I am trying to live with integrity by modeling being open and honest about my feelings and myself. I am also taking on this in my relationship with my boyfriend which is very different from my relationship with my ex-husband.

What steps do I need to take to confront what holds me back?

I need to move through my fears and use my fears to thrust me into motion. I need to grab hold of the fear and bring it with me in motion. I need to step into my greatness with the understanding that opportunities are in the moment and do not necessarily repeat themselves.

What role do I play in holding back the growth of my family and myself?

The role I play is not modeling the behavior I want and expect in myself. By holding back myself because of fear and by holding on to the anger from the past, I continue to live in my own self-torment. I have to move through the anger of all that was. It is the past and living in the pain, and the hurt makes it a part of my future, a future full of repeating the pain. I have got to push through and move forward. All that was, was.

How am I a leader in the family?

By setting the example of how I want my children to live life, I am beginning to model love and being loving by saying "I love you" more, spending time talking about my feelings, kissing and hugging them more, and trying to model ways of sharing truth and being truthful.

I call it integrity and they are starting to understand it when we speak about being honest and truthful about our feelings.

How am I a follower?

Sometimes in my listening, as I learn to be still and let things happen, I hear my children saying things that are profound and worthy for me to change my approach to what is happening at that time or in my life or my family's life. I also do this with my boyfriend. He is very excited about events and decisions. When he is displaying that anxiety, I stop listening and start reacting. When I am still, I am able to hear his points and make choices about where they fit or don't fit me. I move away from my anger or despair and into my truth and my love.

What attributes of mine help and what attributes of mine hinder my leadership?

I want to fix problems and I don't like confrontation. I will rush to get the answer before letting my children and my boyfriend figure it out. I don't like being yelled at, but I do a lot of yelling. I will choose harmony when confrontation is in front of me. I cope with confrontational situations by saying whatever the person wants to hear to get them away from me.

The attribute that helps me is my determination and my need to stay in truth.

Who or what in the family inspires me to pursue my best?

My seventeen-year-old daughter inspires me as I watch her grow and work through her struggles. I get so inspired by watching her step into her life with courage and pain. I get inspired when she expresses her feelings about her dad and her friends. I watch her openly struggle when sharing her emotions with me. I want to be just like her when I grow up. I am trying to learn to openly share my emotions at the moment or shortly after feeling them. I am still screaming silently inside my internal closets of memories. Slowly, I am peeling away at the silence and choosing open aggression instead of passive aggression, like my mother. My bet is I will be at my best when I am fully expressed and uninhibited by fears of aggression, confrontation, and being hurt.

What am I learning about myself?

I am learning to take care of myself. I am learning to find out what matters to me. I am learning to take risks and move forward even when my stomach tenses and my heart skips a beat. I am learning to keep moving into my fears.

I continue to learn that I am the parent, my children need my direction, and they need me to be the parent. This is a role that I am still in motion with because I am being taught to play the role of parent despite my guilt over divorcing their father, being a single parent, and working too much. Even with the guilt, I am learning to hold onto what I know in my gut. I am learning to hold onto what my gut says is right, not what I feel guilty about, and not necessarily what my children want or think of me.

What am I struggling with right now?

I am continuing to discover myself—what I like and don't like; how I struggle with integrity and honesty and avoid using the truth to manipulate and control situations. My struggle is to live everyday with integrity and honesty, push myself to my God, give excellence, and learn to grab my fears and move through them.

Attitude that is productive that carries the most weight…

Go for it … I like taking on new tasks. I love the thrill of new projects that carry some meaning for the community in the form of nonprofits.

I like trying on new approaches with my significant other as well as my children. Sometimes, I try to treat each approach as a learning experience. If it works, I incorporate it, if it doesn't work, I work through it and learn from it. Sometimes, I am greatly disappointed, but I like trying to figure out the challenge.

I am doing more taking risks and stepping out on faith. This has allowed me to try on new things. As a result, I am discovering more things about me. It is my looking back on my past that motivates me to change.

Inspirations from Hyde School, *Nadine Stair, an 85-year-old Kentucky woman wrote: "If I had my life to live over, I'd dare to make more mistakes next time. I'd relax. I'd limber up. I would be sillier than I have this time. I would take fewer things seriously. I would take more chances. I would make more trips. I would climb more mountains and swim more rivers. I would eat more ice cream and fewer beans. I would perhaps have more actual troubles, but I'd have fewer imaginary ones.*

You see, I am one of the people who lived sensibly and sanely, hour after hour, day after day. Oh, I've had my moments, and if I had it to do over again, I'd have nothing else. Just moments one after another, instead of living so many years ahead of each day.

I've been one of those people who never goes anywhere without a thermometer, a hot water bottle, a raincoat, and a parachute. If I had it to do over again, I would travel lighter than I have.

If I had my life to live over, I would start barefoot earlier in the spring and I would stay that way later in the fall. I would go to more dances. I would ride more merry-go-rounds. I would pick more daisies."

I'll do it tomorrow... As I get older, I am getting more tired and where I was comfortable with staying on a task to the wee hours of the night, now I find that as my significant other says, "My mind may say yes but my body won't go along with the program."

The problem is that I have not adjusted the number of tasks to my newly discovered imposed age deficiency. This is becoming a problem. I either need to hire someone, contract out some of my tasks, or become more selective about the quality and cost instead of the number of projects. I will do it later as part of the failure to reevaluate the number of tasks and the dollars associated with them. I remain in denial. It is easier to run from everything than to take a deep look at myself.

As I began to talk during the last exercise, I found that I spent too much time on the task and the quantity/quality of the task than on myself. I have returned to task as a sense of work. I have not spent equal time on my personal development. I want a positive attitude that reflects on me and not on job responsibilities or family needs. I need to have a positive attitude toward self-discovery. I need to get into my physical fitness, my diet, and my hobbies. I need to explore my own happiness, but this is something I have known. I used the fact that I am a single parent as armor, a shield for why I need to do so many things, instead of a reason to take care of myself. This stems from my childhood, always taking care of everyone and never being held accountable for caring for me.

What/who is the wicked witch in my life?

My mechanical self, lacking emotion, lacking self-doubt, and eagerness to take on new ventures is the wicked witch in my life.

Whenever I want a change in my life, I move to my mechanical self. In that self, I sabotage my relationships with the people closest to me. I don't show emotional love and I avoid affection. When I am asked to justify my behavior, I go into complete denial. I began to question the asker's love for me and the need for them in my life. If I cannot shove them out of my life, I blame them for my behavior. I feel removed from my body. I don't like the person that I become but I can't stop the behavior when I am in that zone.

What do I need to do to face this?

I need to face my fears about love and loving. I need to invite my loved ones into my entire world, not just the compartment I keep them in or out of. I need to strengthen my ability to receive love. I need to keep myself in the truth of all my actions and not be afraid to show all of myself. I know the mechanical side of me is my strength, but it is also my weakness. I need to learn to communicate my fears when the mechanical side of me is breaking down and the loving side of me is too weak and scared to reach out for hugs and affection. I need to learn to say I am scared and I need your help and your love.

What new insights am I discovering about myself and my family?

I am discovering the core reason for my avoidance of conflict and why I choose harmony over truth. I am also discovering why I dislike writing things down and why I choose verbal communication over written communication.

New Insights

I am discovering that my children need my emotions. They need a relationship with me that is not just based on things and my aspirations for them. They need to have an emotional touchy-feely relationship with me. I need to develop tools and set goals with my children that will help us, together, to achieve an emotional, loving relationship. I need to share the truth with my children.

What old issues do I need to take action on? What will I do?

One of my old issues is that I have a need to take care of people whom I love and have feelings for. I need to take care of people in a way that handicaps them and me. I fear loved ones will leave me with no warning.

What will I do?

I will begin by telling the truth, choosing truth over harmony. I will begin to listen to my inner feelings and gut reactions and just say "no" when I do not have the means or just simply do not want to do what they are asking of me. I will not create gray areas for harmony. I will start trying to discover myself and my likes and dislikes. I will find what brings me pleasure outside of being a caregiver to everyone. I need to let go of constantly caring for others and start taking care of myself. I will learn to put myself first and to care for myself.

I will open up to my loved ones and let them begin loving me without meaning. I will show them love through emotion: hugs, kisses, and loving words.

I will grab my kids and give them random hugs and kisses. I will say I love you to them every day. I will communicate more with my older children through regular phone calls, emails, or cards.

With my two oldest children, I need to get over the feeling that they will abandon me and choose to love them and be a part of their lives.

Another Letter to Myself

> Hi, Lomenka,
>
> Here we go again, opening Pandora's box of unpleasantness and secrets. I wonder if you will ever be less. You show so many qualities of leadership but it's like a faucet that you turn on and there is only hot

water running. When you are engaged, you are fully engaged. You bet on the truth, but you live in dishonesty when it comes to your heart. When challenged, you will trust people to care enough to tell you the truth, but you are willing to live in dishonesty until you find the courage to move on. The problem is your courage to face situations of the heart is lacking. You will take risks with honesty only when you have fully calculated the risk and have determined the odds. The odds must always be in your favor. It's safe inside your private self. No one is invited in unless they beat the odds. There is no risk-taking, no gambling, and there are a lot of dishonesty to keep loved ones in and the public out.

Free tickets to enter your private world are given to a select few. Everyone else must earn a ticket. You will do everything to keep them at bay before they earn their spot in your heart. Once they are in, you will do all to keep them a secret part of your private haven. Your heart is yearning for more. It wants to remove the entry doors and share your hidden treasure with the public. Your heart wants to share your happiness, but you are just not sure. Your love is private and sacred, but it feels so phony and unreal to live dual lives. So, what are you going to do?

There are some solutions to this dilemma. You can just be free. You can unlock the doors. You can shout your love from the highest mountain. You can begin to celebrate your gift from God of love. You can have the light that shines in your heart shine outside. You can accept the challenge of moving your relationships forward and trust and have faith that they will work themselves out. It is all your choice. Remember to trust in God, have faith, and take a risk. Your love for your partner and your family is not an accident. There are no accidents. God plans all. Trust, be honest, and have faith. Jump into your life. Jump! Jump!

MY POEM

Life is full of choices
Honesty and Courage must be your choice above all.
Love like there is no tomorrow
Have Faith God conquers all.

Comments from others I shared my letter with ...

"You are a unique person that has given me inspiration to express my own feelings."

"Bet on more truth—You are a remarkable woman who deserves love."

"You have a gift of being able to be challenging and supportive at the same time— a born leader who resonates with passion."

"I noted this weekend that you are the only person of color here. I'm disappointed with that. Your determination and charity are admirable, but your heart is an inspiration."

"As someone who has experienced a lot of frustration with my difficulty in finishing projects in nonprofits, I felt inspired and challenged by your optimism and determination."

"Love conquers all—live in it and get all wet. Let your family experience your joy and they will realize the benefit from a whole happy parent."

"There is a quail in your voice that seems 'unreal' to me. Maybe 'head over heart.'"

"I see a power and strength in your seventeen-year-old daughter that I don't 'get' from you. Are you betting on that part of yourself? Since your daughter has it, I know you do also. Are you leading and inspiring?"

"Your passion and clarity are really inspirational. Add the emotional honesty to it and there is no stopping you."

"Are you worried that if you bring this relationship into the open that you will have to take the 'next step'? Life is for living—fully open! —fully alive!"

"You are very articulate and clear on so many things. You are integrating your outer and inner selves in a beautiful way. Stay vulnerable, be even more conscious, and God bless you."

"It's wonderful that you are giving to the community—treasure that."

"Commitment to a loved one can deeply enhance the relationship"

"Let truth be your primary guide."

"Our paths are so similar with partners. I have found that 'baby steps' work best."

"It is so wonderful that you help so many people. Community is key and you have that key, so exalt your personal life."

"It is wonderful to love and be loved—make no apologies and don't look to your children for approval. That was my mistake."

"You are so much more aware, the 2nd time, that you don't have to worry. Trust your heart."

"Follow your heart."

"Allow yourself to enjoy fully."

I found that I had not done anything with the comments after the weekend of sharing thoughts about myself with others. I left the comments in the carry bag I used for the retreat for one month. I was somewhat embarrassed when asked to reflect on the comments that I had not thought about. As I started to prepare for this meeting, I had an "aha" moment. I felt more satisfaction since the retreat as that helped me generate the letter and my recent work with "nonprofits" because what I got was that my work is a part of me. I live and breathe the work I do. I help to facilitate, to empower, and improve communities. I get discouraged by the slow payments, the challenge around my personal finances, and the fear of retaliation from entities like the federal government, especially when I am working to save an organization from folding and the nonprofit is so far from compliance with the law. But I know I have a gift of helping that takes me beyond my fears and pushes me to success for them and a sense of accomplishment for me. I love the feeling of giving back. The love I feel and have for building communities is more powerful than my fears. The affirmations for the weekend reaffirmed and re-energized my commitment to my work.

The loving part of my life, my inner self, is still ruling. The reading of the comments was an "aha" moment that moved me to display my boyfriend's picture on my mirror of family pictures. I have taken baby steps toward my outer self by trying to display my loving inner self to my children. With my boyfriend, I am just practicing expressing my inner feelings in truth and not holding back—even when I have great fears about what I predict or perceive as the outcome. You see, I haven't let go of my fears. I am just trying to slowly push through learning to speak from my heart and not my fears.

THE DILEMMA

By Unknown Author

To laugh is to risk appearing a fool.

To weep is to risk appearing sentimental.

To reach out to another is to risk involvement.

To expose feelings is to risk rejection.

To place your dreams before the crowd is to risk ridicule.

To love is to risk not being loved in return.

To go forward in the face of overwhelming odds is to risk failure.

But risks must be taken because the greatest hazard in life is to risk nothing.

The person, who risks nothing, is nothing.

He may avoid suffering and sorrow, but he cannot team, feel, change, grow, or love.

Chained by his certitudes, he is a slave. He has forfeited his freedom.

Only a person who takes risks is free.

The Invitation by Oriah Mountain Dreamer, "It doesn't interest me what you do for a living. I want to know what you ache for, and if you dare to dream of meeting your heart's longing.

"It doesn't interest me how old you are. I want to know if you will risk looking like a fool for love, for your dream, for the adventure of being alive.

"It doesn't interest me what planets are squaring your moon. I want to know if you have touched the center of your own sorrow, if you have been opened by life's betrayals, or have become shriveled and closed from fear of further pain. I want to know if you can sit with pain, mine or your own, without moving to hide it or fade it or fix it.

"I want to know if you can be with joy, mine or your own, if you can dance with wildness and let the ecstasy fill you to the tips of your fingers and toes without cautioning us to be careful, to be realistic, to remember the limitations of being human.

"It doesn't interest me if the story you are telling me is true. I want to know if you can disappoint another to be true to yourself, if you can bear the accusation of betrayal and not betray your own soul, if you can be faithless and therefore trustworthy.

"I want to know if you can see beauty, even when it's not pretty, every day, and if you can source your own life from its presence.

"I want to know if you can live with failure, yours and mine, and still stand on the edge of the lake and shout to the silver of the full moon, 'Yes!'

"It doesn't interest me to know where you live or how much money you have. I want to know if you can get up, after a night of grief and despair, weary and bruised to the bone, and do what needs to be done to feed the children.

"It doesn't interest me to know where or what or with whom you have studied. I want to know what sustains you, from the inside, when all else falls away.

"I want to know if you can be alone with yourself and if you truly like the company you keep in the empty moments."

TO THE ONES I LOVE &
THOSE WHO HAVE LOVED ME

My Significant Other

What do I fear about this relationship?

I fear that it won't last, that love will go away and that he won't marry me, even though I'm afraid of marriage. I fear that he will succumb to his family's need for him to remain single and unattached. I fear my children won't accept the marriage.

What do I love about our relationship?

I love the love he gives me, his ability to change, my ability to be direct and open with him, the way he shows his love, his heart, and my feelings that just won't go away no matter the distance or separation.

Our differences

He is very afraid someone will mess over his money. He is very frugal and tight with money. I am afraid I won't have enough money. I am less tight but very frugal. My finances don't match his. I work with other people's money every day to secure success in their communities that is for a living. He works with his money every day to secure his own interest. He works with the community every day to educate them and provide social facilities. I love to walk all the time for pleasure. He doesn't. He teaches others how to remain physically fit.

Letter to My Ex-husband

Dear X,

My sincere apology—I need to start this letter by apologizing for not knowing myself enough to give you all of me and for not loving myself enough to take the time to know who I really was. I lived a very mechanical life ignoring my emotions. I put formulas together on how much love to give you. I plugged in the holes whenever necessary, subtracting myself by being nasty and filthy when I wanted to avoid your affection, letting that be my way to say no to your affection. I had a formula for being the best mother to our children and when I thought they were equipped enough to go on their own, I pulled my love away. I lived my life with you and our family void of emotion but very clear about raising a good family and what I thought, clear about having a strong marriage. It wasn't until our next oldest daughter began to spiral downwards to the urban streets that I began to understand some of my imperfections. Putting her in boarding school, Hyde was the best thing I could have done for both her and me. I thought the school was saving her but in reality, it was saving both of us. Those two and half years in the school made her come back to her senses and made me grow up. You see, I was stuck in the past, in my childhood. I never forgave or forgot how my anger was so devastating and destructive that it stopped my dad from saying goodbye before he left this earth. You see, both things silenced me. They were my emotional bondage that not even you nor could our family release me from. My intelligence was my best friend. I was always very creative and innovative. I knew how to always think out of the box. While I was void of emotion, I was equipped with intelligence.

I was not prepared for a marriage or a husband. The blessings were our five children. They were my salvation. Each child was a confirmation that I could make a difference. I could take my screwed-up childhood and my dysfunctional parents and turn it around with my children. I had a chance to start over again. A new canvas, a new start, I could show my parents how to do it right.

As for you, I loved your smile, your intellect, and your love of family and children. Today, I am not sure if I ever really loved you, but I am sure in those eighteen years of our relationship, I was one hundred percent committed to you and our family. Thank you for hanging out all those years and continuing to support our children emotionally.

I could say a lot of negative things, but this is a healing letter. The past was the past and my future's so much brighter than my anger. Today, I understand myself enough to understand love. Probably because I love me. I love all that took place to bring me to this person I can stare at in the mirror and say I am great, I am wonderful, and I am beautiful. I am loving my life and I could not have arrived here without my past. So, thank you for the experiences and the growth.

Your Ex-Wife

My Letter to My Oldest Two Children

To My Oldest Two Children,

I never liked the term stepmother. So, I use what fits best for me, which is my adopted children. You are children in my life that did not come through me but are part of me. I chose you the moment you stepped into my San Francisco apartment. You knocked over the bookshelves in my apartment and I could see the fear on your face. I wondered how I could yell at such beautiful children. I was in love with you from that moment on.

I have to apologize to you for my lack of parenting skills, but I guess no one really knows the right way to parent. I think we just go about the business of not trying to recreate our parents' mistakes with them but that leaves the rest of our parenting by instinct. My instincts were as real as my love for you. Since I know love sometimes hurts, I am as guilty as my parents were with me, with bad parenting. As I reflect on our times. I know this is true and I apologize. There was never any malice in my heart, just a lot of old baggage that I never reconciled before marrying your father.

I knew by education the right way to raise children but my own insecurities from my childhood got in the way. Even now, while I loved every moment I spent with you while raising you today, our communication is lacking. When we talk, I am still Mom and you are still my children. I want more but I don't know how to go after a better relationship. I am left with the fear of having pushed you away to keep you from hearing the truth about me, the truth that I kept suppressed from me down deep in my soul for self-protection. I was sexually abused by my brother, and I believed through my anger I kept my father from saying his last goodbyes before he died. While I say these things with very little emotion today, during our years together as a family, I was not so free to speak about this, not because I was told not to but because I could not accept my childhood sexual abuse, so I pretended it did not happen. I wanted it to go away. I thought the older I got, the more the experience would disappear in my life, almost like watching the gray hairs slowly take over while the black hairs disappear. What I learned is that the memories of the past don't disappear. They just manifest themselves in new personality traits and behaviors in you. As for me, I never wanted to get too close to anyone, not even your father or you because I knew I would lose you, just like I lost my dad. You would walk out on me and never say a word, just leave. So, I felt the best way to protect myself was to never let anyone all the way in. I loved you deeply, but I couldn't show it because I knew you would hurt me. You had a mother to run to and I always knew that you could leave me any day and choose a life with her. It never stopped me from loving you. I loved you more than my own life and sometimes, you pushed me to show that. But those moments only came when I needed to honor my love over my fears.

To my daughter, I wanted to leave your father before I did but I made a promise to you that I would keep our family together and that I would always be there for you. I will honor the promise of always being there for you until I leave this earth. To honor you, I stayed with your father until you were old enough to be on your own. I felt that one divorce in a child's life was enough. I was about my family.

To my son, I never knew a day when you weren't my son. I raised you like my son and you will die being my son. You hardly ever communicated with your natural mom when you lived with us. I always remember asking you to call her. Once you got on the phone, you were great but initiating the phone call was always hard for you. Now, I am receiving the same treatment. I love you and I will always love you. Communication works both ways. I need to release my fears and start calling you and not just wait for you to call me.

To both of you, I love you more than my own life. I am sorry for being so emotionless through your childhood. I wish I could go back and do more of what I am doing today with your younger brother and sister, which is saying I love you at least once a day, randomly stopping to hug and kiss them out of the blue and speaking out of honesty and integrity as much as I can. I am finally loving myself enough to forgive people in my past and move on with my future because I have learned to love myself, it makes it easier to love them and you. I have to let go of my fear of the past of all that you think of me for what I didn't do and move on to loving you and my grandchildren. It is hard for me to make this turn but I promise you I will. The one lesson I have learned in my older years is that fear should never run or rule your actions.

I love you. Please take care of your partners and my grandchildren.

Love,
Mom

My Letter to My Oldest Brother

To My Oldest Brother,

I tried to forget those nights when I was afraid of the dark and I would creep into your bed for safety. I was a little girl afraid of the bogeyman. I was looking for solace, safety, and comfort from the dark. I used to see dead people. I would dream of people dying and in their caskets. After a few months, it was like déjà vu; they would die. I remember when dad's cousins died one after the other and it was almost as if I could see it in my dreams before their deaths happened. I would tell grandma about my dreams, and she would listen and say that happens to some people. I was afraid to sleep at night. I remember it like it was yesterday being upstairs in the room we shared with no one but me and I was on my knees praying when I felt someone sit next to me. I thought it was you or Walter scaring me again but as I went to yell at you, there was nobody there. There was no one on the steps leading to our room either. I let it go and began praying again. I felt the same thing this time. I looked over my pillow and I saw an imprint on my pillow like someone was sitting next to me. I ran downstairs and I remember Mom telling me it wasn't anything, just my imagination. Again, I told grandma what happened, and she said sometimes, spirits pick certain people to talk to. I told her I didn't want it to be me. I then began to pray to God to have the spirits come to me in my dreams and not appear in any other form. I accepted the dreams about people's deaths and caskets. I would tell Grandma since she was the only one who would listen. You, our younger brother, and Mom thought I was crazy and making stuff up. Later in life, as I became a teenager, I just began to accept some of my dreams about the future. People call them déjà vu. I was okay until I dreamt about our father's death. I saw him in the casket. I told Mom and she said, "Dreams don't necessarily mean anything. For the first month, I watched Dad like a hawk." After a little time passed, I shrugged it off. He died about six months later. I started praying harder to God and to Dad. I begged Dad to only come to me in my dreams and not as a spirit talking to me. I told him and God I was afraid of spirits and I didn't want that to happen. Shortly after his death, I began having dreams of Dad talking to me, showing me he was okay, and almost guiding me through college and helping me make choices. I saw myself at Stony Brook University in the dorms before I selected that school as my four-year college. Once I went to college, my dreams turned into study tools. If I studied a problem long enough and went to sleep with it in my mind, I would awake in the night or the morning with the answer. There was more to my life as a child than just being scary. It did not help that you and my brother loved to force me to watch scary movies with you while Mom was at Bingo and with all the lights out. Then you would pretend to go to the bathroom and stay away for a while and when I went to find you, you would jump out of nowhere and scare me.

Anyway, that was who I was. I was scared of my own shadow. Instead of you pushing me out of bed like our younger brother did, you would turn over and begin to feel all over me, my breast, and dig in my private parts. You were six years older than me and you knew it was wrong. Soon, you began to call me to your bed and like a young fool, I would respond because I knew when I was scared the next time, you would not let me sleep with you. When you heard Mom coming to check on us, you would push me out of your bed and send me back to mine. One time, I was out on the next-door neighbor's stoop with you and some of your older friends and I heard you and one of your friends bragging about what you were doing to me in the night. I heard your friend talking about how he was doing it to his girl cousin too. I felt ashamed and embarrassed. I began writing to Mom to tell her what was going on and asking her for my own room. She ignored my letters and pretended she did not know what was going on. I continued to write to her about what was happening and she continued to ignore my letters. Soon after Dad came home to live, that's when you stopped.

I was a child looking for safety and you took advantage of me. I knew it was wrong, but I had it twisted. I thought as long as I felt safe, I would let you do whatever you needed to do to me. I knew it was wrong, but I didn't know how to change it. I had mixed emotions. Being touched felt different and strange but being scared was a heavier and stronger emotion. I never understood why Mom thought that two older sons and her younger daughter could co-exist in one room, especially with a son that was six years older than her daughter, a teenager with hormones out of control.

I began working with Grandma to ask Mom and Dad about moving to a bigger house. Dad began to tell me the stories about wanting to move and Mom not being willing to move. I was stunned. I was young but very precocious and extremely mature. I was forced to grow up before my time.

I would escape to Grandma's house every summer to get away from our room. Even there, there was sexual molestation going on. Dad's youngest brother, our uncle, would ask girls to sit on his lap while he felt all over our private parts and his son was no better. This time, I spoke up and told Grandma. She lit into and he never touched me again. I don't know what happened with the rest of my cousins, but I was getting stronger and I wasn't going to let that happen to me anymore.

I was so happy when you went away to college. You were eighteen and I was twelve. Even though the molestation stopped when you got a steady girlfriend and Dad came home, I was happy to see you leave.

When you started having babies and they were girls, I remember cringing at the thought of what you may be doing to them. I pray you grew out of it, but I just didn't know. I never liked being around you too much. It was always strange and weird. It was helpful that Dad did not like your wife because it meant you weren't hanging around the house a lot. I liked your first wife, but I could never get too close to her because it meant I had to be close to you. I never forgave or forgot what happened between us. I just suppressed it.

Today, I will call you when there is an emergency with our family. I called you when I was in a deep mess with my job and I needed help from my family. I haven't grown a relationship of social conversations between a brother and a sister.

I had an opportunity to meet with my youngest niece while she was here with her Mom in California at a conference. I apologized for my aloof behavior, and I shared the truth of your and my relationship with her. I wanted her to know I was distant for a reason. She was a college graduate at the time and astute enough to know that my surface discussion wasn't the reason. It felt good to finally reveal the truth. I also felt good because several years ago, I wrote you a letter similar to this one stating the same things I am stating today.

Today, I forgive you because we were kids. I also forgive myself for being a child who knew better but had no real voice. I forgive myself for settling for the best solution to my fears. I accept that children don't always make good decisions and adults don't always want to hear a child's voice. I forgive you because if I don't, I will continue to allow your acts of sexual molestation to take over my ability to be a fully functioning loving and sexually healthy adult. My forgiveness of you allows me to love fully with no regrets. I forgive you because I forgive myself. I love me. My past is just the past, it does not and will not make my tomorrow.

With Love
Your Sister

My Letter to My Grandmother

Hi, Grams,

I have no apologies and remorse but a lot of gratitude and thanks. You listened when I didn't understand how to ask God to be my friend and my provider. You listened when no one else would. While I did not start out trying to model my life after you, I did. You were a silent strength that mastered her universe by simply moving through and taking no prisoners along the way. If there were pairs in your life, I never saw them in your eyes. You spoke and walked through life with quiet wisdom and command over your life and your destiny. You lived your belief and faith in God. You displayed this to me with your quiet wisdom. I can't remember hearing your voice raise higher than a normal octave but yet, you raised those five hardheaded boys and had the nerve to adopt a girl. You were and still are my hero. You rescued me when I was drowning in a sea of despair, and you taught me how to hold on when I thought there was nothing left. You helped me develop a quiet inner strength that is with me in my life today. Your courage was translated to me through your actions. I never fear what is ahead. I embraced it. Instead, with a sense of calmness, as if it is just a part of what I do. Thank you for teaching me about life and how to struggle through difficulties and know that it will be alright. You taught me that life is worth embracing even through the trials.

The trips that we took together, you, I, and your best friend were awesome. They opened my eyes to the world. We would speed down the highway and travel the mountains with quiet bliss and a sense of adventure and loss. I still remember seeing the cars and trucks on the mountain trip to West Virginia laid out on the road, jack- knifed, I was terrified, but your best friend, my aunt, kept on driving like we were in a hurry to die as I am sure some of those passengers in the jack-knifed rigs did. But we kept on trucking up the hill at about eighty or ninety miles an hour. All I could think of is that I am with my grandmother and she won't let anything happen to me, so I convinced myself to relax. I loved the game you and Auntie would play with me, making me tell you what each sign said on the road before we passed it. Every summer, I would look forward to one of our trips whether it was to the South or on a bus to see your sister in D.C. I didn't care as long as I was with you. Although D.C. was not my favorite trip because your sister had too many roaches and as soon as we turned on the light, they were like wallpaper all over the walls, I would cover my ears when I slept because I did not want a roach to crawl in my ears, but Auntie made some great quilts. She would pull out her scrap bag and begin quilting as you sat and talked. I did not mind those times because, during the day, the roaches weren't as bad as at night.

Auntie was old, she was in her nineties, blind, and somewhat dead, but she knew you and you both would just sit and talk, and I would listen to the old stories and watch her quilt. I remember you collecting scraps of material in garbage bags to take to her. To this day, I don't know how we carried everything on the Greyhound bus. You were so small in stature, and I wasn't much in size at that time. I was barely nine or ten years old, but we did it. It always seemed like Auntie was sitting by the window waiting for us when we arrived. I would not trade those moments for all the money in the world.

Grandma, you exposed me to so much without me understanding the value of your silent lessons. I was your heart and you were mine. Today, I look up toward heaven and thank God for sending me an angel in my life. I hope I am all you expected because I know you were all I expected and what I needed in my life. I love you, Grandma, and I will always love you.

With Love and Admiration,
Your Granddaughter

MY CHILDREN

How do I feel about my seventeen-year-old child's success?

As I watch her grow beyond her street life experiences which were dirty and ugly, I feel overly excited but somewhat subdued. I am sometimes waiting for the element of negative surprise that will dampen her successes and return me to the old place of worry and sadness. My daughter has come a long way and I am grateful to her school, God, and her for all her accomplishments. I can't wait to see what the future holds for her as she begins to put her past behind her. She has some real tools now that she and I can both draw on. I know she will make mistakes after all I did but now, she knows where to find the answers. Her new self is strong and committed.

How do I handle the struggles and failures of my seventeen-year-old child?

I respond out of my head, my intellect. I secondly respond from my emotions and sense of honesty and integrity for myself. I don't like some of the choices she makes but I can't control her choices. The irony for me is that I want to stop her pain before it happens, but I am not in control of her destiny. Only she and God can control her fate. I have come to the conclusion that it is my job to steer her in a direction away from harm based on my life experiences and to challenge her to live a morally correct life. Also, for me, I must stand for something and teach her to stand for something and then let her make her own choices. I am sometimes hurt and disappointed but most times, I love the way she cleans up her mistakes.

Have I ever tried to manipulate the outcome of my children's potential failures?

All the time, but I am learning to listen more—take a stand in my own convictions, provide controls, and wait. The wait now lets me stand in my convictions and my control in terms of repercussions for actions inconsistent with my convictions as a parent. I have learned to state the concern, provide consequences, and wait and have faith that my child will make the right decision. I do a whole lot of praying while I am waiting.

Have my children seen me fail at any time?

Yes, at my marriage to their father. Yes, at my job choices. Yes, at my business choice. I feel hard with my choices made on my job and the choices I have made with different business ventures. I was publicly humiliated and so were my children. We survived. I believe we live a better life today. They saw me hold on to my faith while they watched my tears and my pain. I held to my stand that God never gives you more than you can bear. I reminded them as I reminded myself to hold on tight to their faith and always stand for what is right. God never fails the believers.

What attitudes hold me back from going after my best?

My fear of success—my fear of being publicly evaluated by strangers and held to standards that are not my own. My sense of privacy—I like having my family life be mine and not shared with others. I want protection from very public life for my children. I am challenged with the lack of ability to say "no" out loud to people who want to intrude on my personal affairs. For me, success and fame are linked. This book is an open challenge for me to push through my fears.

What is my biggest personal issue?

My biggest personal issue is learning to say "no" in my business and still have people/clients value my worth. My goal is to set my fees and hold onto them. My flexibility should only occur when I have run the numbers and it makes sense for my bottom line. My bottom line must include my family budget, my savings, and my reserve of three months' worth of expenses as a contingency, a backup.

I also need to let go of the outcome. If my clients say no, I can't afford you, accept that and not make it a form of personal rejection. I must value the job and the commitment to my clients by holding myself to high standards and my own integrity—being honest when I need to change the due dates, being honest about my schedule, and being honest about the amount of time that goes into completing the task.

How will I do this?

I must double my time commitment because I always think that tasks take less time than they really do.

I must be honest about shifting the timelines when it doesn't work for me.

I must stay in communication with my clients.

I must honor my values.

I need to recognize and consider if necessary, renegotiating my commitments with my current clients.

I must constantly review my client base over time and drop my clients that do not pay on my current pay scale.

All new clients must be evaluated by the following criterion: my time, my hourly rate, and my ability to cover my expenses.

What is my budget? I need to know my monthly expenses, my annual expenses, my wish list, my budget and timelines for the business, and my future three to five-year goals.

I need to get organized, set some goals, and keep track of everyday finances.

What are our family's biggest issues?

Money and my children's father/my ex-husband.

Money?

My son's fees for football and basketball leagues and birthday gifts for friends. My youngest daughter needs more clothes. My seventeen-year-old has school expenses, college application fees, travel, living expenses, and clothes. I need to maintain a positive cash flow, pay off outstanding debts, and repurchase my house.

Father/my ex-husband

My son wants more communication between me and his father. He is worried about a lack of money to do more. He is worried about how much money we have—no child support.

My youngest daughter wants more communication between me and her father and she is worried about how much money we have—no child support. We have hit the money jar a few times.

My seventeen-year-old is afraid of true in-your-face communication with me and her father. She wants to break her battle with harmony, keep the peace, and move toward integrity and honesty. She is worried about how much money we have, no child support. She has gone without a lot of things other students have.

My issue is that I need to let go of the hatred toward my ex-husband and move toward forgiving. I have to drop what I want him to be and move toward who and what he is. I have to move toward letting go of the hurt, the pain, the betrayal, the hatred, and the disgust, forgive him for who he is, and know that I cannot change him. I just need to accept it and let go of the hatred.

How are my family and my issues connected?

By holding on to my hatred for my ex-husband and I am still holding on to our old relationship. I am still settling for the crumbs. I am still not willing to stand up and say I am worth much more. I am stuck in the old me who was in that relationship without a voice but manipulating from behind the scenes. I have moved the behavior away from my family, but I am still living the behavior in my business life. I keep screaming to get out and to unleash my power over my choices, but each form of rejection sends me back into that ugly eighteen-year marriage where I had no voice. I continue to manipulate from behind the scenes. I have got to forgive my ex-husband and I have got to forgive myself. My mantra.

> *"I am not my ex-husband's wife. I am a businesswoman, an executive, an entrepreneur, a writer and an achiever. I do have a voice and I can be out front and I can say what I want and deliver on my promises."*

> *"I am worth what I ask for and I deliver what I promise."*

My children are stuck because they are modeling some of my behaviors. I believe when I find my voice and soar like an eagle, they will find their voice as well. When I let go of their father, they will embrace him more and forgive me for leaving him.

What is something I need the courage to take hold of?

I need to take hold of control over my business. I need to set clear achievable goals. I need to take hold of the beginning to clear out the old baggage in my life and in my business. I need to start rebuilding with the things that bring me joy, happiness, fulfillment, and aid with achieving my personal and business goals.

I need to set my consultant rates and stick to them. I need to slowly purge my old client base to reflect my current rates. I need to bill my clients in a timely manner. I need to aggressively set limits with my clients. I need to stay within these limits or renegotiate the contract.

What is something I would like to let go of?

I would like to let go of taking clients that do not fit into my fee structure. I would like to let go of feeling guilty about their dollar limitations and not collecting what is owed to me.

I would like to let go of my eighteen-year marriage and take on my new relationship for all that it has to offer without my old baggage weighing me down.

I would like to let go of developing my worth based on the client and instead, set my price and negotiate timelines and payments based on my bottom line.

Who am I?

I am committed to learning to love myself. I want to push beyond my past and learn to embrace it, talk about it, deal with the ones who hurt me and accept it for what it was and move beyond it. It was what it was. I want to discover what I like and what makes me happy, and I want to enjoy my success in life.

Where am I going?

I am reaching for the sky, for my best. I know that I am powerful, and I am not afraid to step into my potential. I am learning to stop looking to others for their approval.

What do you want your life to be about?

I want my life to be about what I gave to the world that is not in neon lights but touches my soul with giving for the sake of giving back. I want my higher power to be able to talk with me on the Day of Judgment and say that I have made good use of the talents He bestowed upon me. I want to live with humility and integrity. I want my children to model my life for their children.

I see myself giving to the world by continuing to work with nonprofit organizations—shore them up, help them to sustain their efforts, and work to develop new nonprofits that are based in communities and provide services to their communities.

I want to write about my journey through life as an urban girl in her memories about her journey. I want to share my story in an effort to help others and provide a sense of purpose for me and hope for others.

Self-Honesty/Truth written by Hyde School: *"If we wish to fulfill our unique potential, our destiny in life, we need the ongoing guidance of conscience. However, as we move closer to our dreams, the more susceptible we become to our fears and insecurities. These negative thoughts color the view we have of our true selves and we then become overly concerned with our present welfare. We allow our egos to control us, undermining the wisdom of conscience and interfering with our true long-term growth needs."*

My goals are to open a Hyde Charter School in Oakland, to write at least three books, to find two things that I love to do that bring me happiness, to stop flying under the radar and move through obstacles by plowing through them, to let go of what people think, to embrace my passion for taking on tasks and loving the thrill of the process of achieving them, and to continue to hit the target loving the focus and dedication that I have through the process. Most of all, I want to walk into my fears and let go of the outcome.

"Our perception is so firmly rooted in our upbringing, that we may not see them as attitudes that we can change. We must begin by the cultivation of our own self-honesty. While we need courage to confront these attitudes, this unburdening will also be a great source of relief. The truth really does set us free."

I have learned that I was still embracing hatred toward my mom. I thought I had forgiven her, but I had not. I also discovered that my inhibitions around writing had a lot to do with my mother not acknowledging my letters. I would write to her as a young, troubled girl. Writing a letter to my mom about my feelings toward her began to free me of some of the hatred I was holding on to. The best experience was taking a risk and reading the letter to my mom face to face. I have moved past the hatred by looking at her as she explained or had no explanation for her actions but more simply, her heartfelt apologies. I now have some understanding of my mom and myself as a mother. I now can say to myself, "It was what it was." The key thing is that these were events of my past, not my future.

As a result of someone saying to me that I use my writing to manipulate others and the reading of my written letter to my mom, I began to learn to love myself and begin writing again.

I need to get honest about my health. I know that diabetes, high blood pressure, and glaucoma are family health issues and are hereditary. My father had two of the three diseases. My mother has all three of them. I became a vegetarian at age twenty to begin to look at my own dietary issues. I am still constantly battling with my weight. I know that maintaining a healthy weight is a large factor in the prevention of high blood pressure and diabetes. I know this but I still overeat. I don't eat because I'm hungry. I eat because food provides me comfort. When I am worried or extremely excited, I resort to eating. Until I can find a resolution to the problem, I use food to comfort me. I eat fast and I eat a lot.

Consequences if I don't get honest:

I continue to beat myself up about being overweight and I eat out of frustration. I do not control my overeating habits. Right now, I am healthy. I will have high blood pressure and have to take medicines to control my blood pressure. I will end up with diabetes and have to take insulin—shoot myself with needles—and monitor my sugar levels daily. Once this cycle of disease takes place, there is no getting rid of it.

If I get honest:

I will be happy with my physical appearance. I will possibly avoid hypertension and diabetes. I will be a healthier person. I will learn another way of dealing with my anxiety. I will start by learning to love myself.

LETTER OF GROWTH
WRITTEN BY ME TO ME

Dear Lomenka,

I am your private self finally having an opportunity to speak to you. You keep speaking about this relationship with your boyfriend. You only speak about the relationship in a safe, protected space and with your 17-year-old daughter. You are afraid to reveal your relationship to your former co-workers who know you both so well. You fear their comments and their jokes. You neither have nor even told your children who live with you and their older siblings that you are in a relationship and that you have a boyfriend. You are so afraid of their feelings. You don't want them to remove the high place, the pedestal, that they have you on. You are to them a single Muslim mom who doesn't need the love of a man to survive. So, for that reason, you don't ask or demand full disclosure of your relationship to the world.

Your public self loves the idea of living within the mandates of Islam. It's safe. Being the perfect woman who does not bring a man into her bed in front of her children is correct and therefore, the relationship is no one's business but yours and his. Your public self wants and requires the marriage, the wedding, and the ring to feel right about you and to be accepted by the world. Inside your heart, both your public and private self just want the love and affection of a man, your man. Both selves want to be truthful with family, friends, and the world in general but in order for this to happen, you have to decide to stop battling between both selves. You have to decide whether your image is more important than your heart. You have to break the stereotypes and images you have set up with your family, friends, religious community, and former co-workers. You have to take a risk. Your private self loves just being with your boyfriend and discovering new ways to be in a loving relationship with a man. Let go of your fears about your children's reaction to a man that is so different from their dad. Forget about your fears of being challenged by friends who know you and my say that he is not good enough for you. Release your fear of your boyfriend not being able to handle public scrutiny. You have met his family. The truth is you don't know if you are strong enough to be placed under the public microscope yet another time. You know that your kids have gone thru a lot with your divorce from their father. You are not sure if you want to introduce another relationship with a man yet. Take a risk! Stop living behind the door. It's alright to be wrong but being safe is boring. Reach for the stars and if you don't make it, keep trying and reaching. Your past was painful, but you get to define your future. Reach for your happiness with no regrets. Learn from the past and keep pushing through. You are worth it and if he is worth anything and the relationship is powerful enough, great things will happen. If not, keep taking risks until you find that powerful exciting love but don't hide and don't be ashamed. The past is over. It's your life—live it!

I Love You,
Your Private & Public Self

www.ingramcontent.com/pod-product-compliance
Lightning Source LLC
Chambersburg PA
CBHW031529120626
46545CB00005B/2065